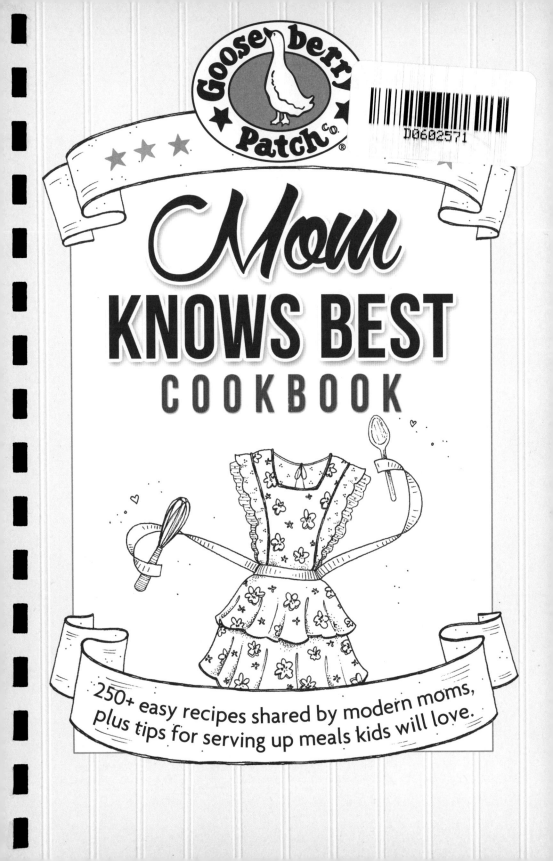

Gooseberry Patch Co.

Mom
KNOWS BEST
COOKBOOK

250+ easy recipes shared by modern moms, plus tips for serving up meals kids will love.

Gooseberry Patch
2545 Farmers Dr., #380
Columbus, OH 43235

www.gooseberrypatch.com

1•800•854•6673

Copyright 2014, Gooseberry Patch 978-1-62093-154-7
First Printing, October, 2014

U.S. to Metric Recipe Equivalents

Volume Measurements

1/4 teaspoon	1 mL
1/2 teaspoon	2 mL
1 teaspoon	5 mL
1 tablespoon = 3 teaspoons	15 mL
2 tablespoons = 1 fluid ounce	30 mL
1/4 cup	60 mL
1/3 cup	75 mL
1/2 cup = 4 fluid ounces	125 mL
1 cup = 8 fluid ounces	250 mL
2 cups = 1 pint =16 fluid ounces	500 mL
4 cups = 1 quart	1 L

Weights

1 ounce	30 g
4 ounces	120 g
8 ounces	225 g
16 ounces = 1 pound	450 g

Oven Temperatures

300° F	150° C
325° F	160° C
350° F	180° C
375° F	190° C
400° F	200° C
450° F	230° C

Baking Pan Sizes

Square

8x8x2 inches	2 L = 20x20x5 cm
9x9x2 inches	2.5 L = 23x23x5 cm

Rectangular

13x9x2 inches	3.5 L = 33x23x5 cm

Loaf

9x5x3 inches	2 L = 23x13x7 cm

Round

8x1-1/2 inches	1.2 L = 20x4 cm
9x1-1/2 inches	1.5 L = 23x4 cm

Contents

Dedication

To families everywhere who agree that the dinner table is the heart of the home.

Appreciation

Thanks to all who shared their very best answers to the question, "What's for dinner?"

Bacon-Egg Cheddar Waffle

Amy Bradsher
Roxboro, NC

We love our BECW! My kids think it's hilarious to eat waffles with their hands, and it always makes them giggle. It's a fun breakfast at home or on the go. Save time...make 'em ahead and freeze!

8 eggs, beaten
1/3 c. milk
4 t. butter, divided

1/2 c. shredded Cheddar cheese, divided
1 lb. bacon, crisply cooked

Whisk eggs and milk together. Melt one teaspoon butter in a small skillet over low heat. Add 1/4 of egg mixture and cook omelet-style; top with 2 tablespoons cheese when nearly done. Repeat, making 3 more omelets. Meanwhile, make Waffles. To assemble sandwiches, slide one omelet between 2 waffles; top with several slices bacon. Slice in half along the waffle's divider lines. Serve immediately, or wrap with wax paper, place in plastic zipping bags and freeze. Serves 4 to 8.

Waffles:

3-1/2 c. white whole-wheat flour
4 eggs, beaten
3 c. buttermilk

1/4 c. butter, melted
2 t. baking soda
1 t. salt

In a large bowl, whisk together all ingredients until smooth. Add batter by 1/2 cupfuls to a preheated waffle iron; cook according to manufacturer's directions. Makes 8 to 12 waffles.

Set the breakfast table the night before...you may even get the kids to help you. Then enjoy a relaxed breakfast in the morning!

Becky's Breakfast Pizza

Becky Drees
Pittsfield, MA

*This recipe is very flexible...use whatever ingredients
you have on hand. Kids love it!*

13.8-oz. tube refrigerated
    pizza dough
5 eggs, beaten
1/4 c. milk
1/4 t. dried oregano
1/8 t. pepper
1 c. cooked ham, chicken, turkey
    or bacon, diced

1-1/2 c. mixed vegetables like
    mushrooms, tomatoes,
    peppers, green onions and
    olives, chopped
1-1/2 c. shredded Cheddar,
    Swiss or mozzarella cheese

Pat dough into the bottom and up the sides of a greased 11"x9" baking
pan or a large springform pan. Bake at 375 degrees for 10 to
12 minutes, until lightly golden. Meanwhile, whisk together eggs,
milk and seasonings in a bowl; carefully pour mixture onto baked
crust. Bake an additional 8 to 10 minutes, until egg mixture is almost
set. Top with your choice of meat, vegetables and cheese. Return to
oven and bake 5 to 10 minutes more, until cheese melts. Let stand
5 minutes before slicing. Makes 8 to 10 servings.

A muffin tin is handy when breakfast time is short. Fill it up
with chopped veggies and cheese for do-it-yourself breakfast
pizzas, or berries and nuts for topping pancakes, waffles and
oatmeal. It can even be filled and refrigerated the night before.

Cream Cheese Pancakes

Patricia Owens
Sullivan, OH

My son and I really enjoy these pancakes. I make all of the pancakes at once, and later he reheats the leftovers for his breakfast. If you'd like to make waffles, just add two tablespoons oil to the batter.

1/2 c. cream cheese
2 T. sugar
1 t. vanilla extract
1 egg, beaten

1-1/2 c. milk
2 c. biscuit baking mix
Optional: 1 c. blueberries

In a microwave-safe large bowl, microwave cream cheese for about 20 seconds, until softened. Add sugar, vanilla and egg; blend well. Add milk and biscuit mix; stir until moistened. Gently fold in blueberries, if using. Pour batter by 1/3 cupfuls onto a greased, heated griddle. Cook on both sides until golden. Makes 8 to 9 pancakes; serves 2 to 3.

Make breakfast fun for kids! Cut the centers from a slice of toast with a cookie cutter, serve milk or juice with twisty straws or put a smiley face on a bagel using raisins and cream cheese.

Grab & Go Breakfasts

Mini Pancake Muffins

Tina Butler
Royse City, TX

These little pancake bites will help school or work mornings run a bit smoother. They're fluffy, a little sweet and taste just like real pancakes. By far our favorites are just plain old buttermilk pancakes, but you can add some chocolate chips or blueberries if you like.

2 c. biscuit baking mix
1 c. buttermilk
1/2 c. pure maple syrup

2 eggs, beaten
Garnish: additional maple syrup

Lightly spray a mini muffin tin with non-stick vegetable spray. In a large bowl, combine biscuit mix, buttermilk, maple syrup and eggs; mix until blended. Pour batter evenly into 24 mini muffin cups, filling nearly to the top of each cup. Bake at 350 degrees for 10 to 12 minutes, until tops are lightly golden and spring back when lightly touched. Cool muffins in tin for 5 minutes; remove to a wire rack. Serve warm, drizzled with maple syrup. To freeze extra muffins, place one inch apart on a baking sheet. Freeze for 20 to 30 minutes, until firm. Transfer to a plastic zipping bag. When ready to serve, reheat in the microwave. Makes 2 dozen.

Waffles and pancakes can be frozen in plastic freezer bags for up to a month. Reheat them in a toaster or microwave for a quick homestyle breakfast on busy weekdays.

Apricot-Almond Cereal Bars

Allison Paschal
Bauxite, AR

*My kids love cereal bars...they gobble them up! This is
my version of a healthier alternative.*

8-oz. pkg. dried apricots,
  finely chopped
3 to 5 T. sugar
1 c. water, divided
2 c. quick-cooking oats,
  uncooked
2/3 c. all-purpose or whole-
  wheat flour

1 c. slivered almonds, divided
1/2 c. brown sugar, packed
1/4 t. salt
1/4 t. nutmeg
1/4 t. cinnamon
6 T. cold butter, sliced
Optional: 3 T. pure maple syrup
  or honey

Combine apricots, sugar and 2/3 cup water in a saucepan. Bring to
a boil over medium heat; reduce heat to low and simmer for 5 to
10 minutes, until soft and slightly syrupy. Remove from heat; cool.
Meanwhile, in a food processor, combine oats, flour, 1/2 cup almonds,
brown sugar, salt and spices. Pulse until blended, about 4 to 6 times.
Add cold butter; process just until crumbly. Add remaining water;
process just until combined. Press 2/3 of oat mixture into the bottom
of a greased 13"x9" baking pan. In a clean food processor, process
cooled apricot mixture to a jelly consistency; spread evenly over crust.
Sprinkle with remaining almonds. Crumble remaining oat mixture over
the top; lightly press in. If desired, drizzle with maple syrup or honey.
Bake at 350 degrees for 25 to 30 minutes, until topping is crisp. Cut
into bars. Makes one dozen.

Kitchen scissors are a handy helper. Grab 'em
to make quick work of cutting up dried fruits...
cut right into the mixing bowl!

Grab & Go *Breakfasts*

Yummy Good Breakfast Bars
Becky Holsinger
Belpre, OH

*These no-bake bars are really easy to make. I'm not usually
a breakfast person, but now that I've tried these, I might eat
breakfast more often! Serve with fresh fruit.*

1-2/3 c. granola cereal
1-2/3 c. bran flake cereal
1-2/3 c. wheat & barley cereal
1 c. berry-flavor gummy fruit
   snack mix

1 c. mini semi-sweet chocolate
   chips
1-1/4 c. creamy peanut butter
3/4 c. honey
3/4 c. brown sugar, packed

Combine cereals, fruit snack mix and chocolate chips in a large
heat-proof bowl; set aside. Combine peanut butter, honey and brown
sugar in a saucepan. Cook and stir over low heat until creamy. Pour
peanut butter mixture over cereal mixture; stir to combine. Press into
a greased 13"x9" baking pan. Cover and chill; cut into squares. Makes
about 1-1/2 dozen.

Crunchy cereal bars are terrific for breakfasts on the go!
Bake a big batch, then wrap each bar separately in plastic wrap
and freeze. Bars will thaw in about one hour, so pull out as
many as you need first thing in the morning.

Breakfast in a Bun

Amy Cassidy
Morganton, NC

A fast way to eat breakfast...wrap it up and eat it on the go!

4 eggs, beaten
1 to 2 T. milk
2 to 3 t. butter
4 hot dog buns, warmed

Optional: 1/4 c. mayonnaise
4 slices American cheese
8 brown & serve breakfast
    sausage links, prepared

Whisk together eggs and milk. In a skillet over low heat, scramble eggs in butter to desired doneness. Meanwhile, spread warmed buns with mayonnaise, if desired; top each bun with one cheese slice and 2 sausage links. Spoon eggs into buns. Serves 4.

Sausage Muffins to Go

Tamela James
Grove City, OH

My daughters were in band, theater and many other school activities. This recipe was always requested when parents were to provide breakfast for the students. My girls' friends loved them!

1/2 lb. ground pork sausage
2 c. all-purpose flour
2 T. sugar
1 T. baking powder
1/4 t. salt

1 c. milk
1 egg, lightly beaten
1/4 c. butter, melted and slightly
    cooled
1/2 c. shredded Cheddar cheese

Brown sausage in a skillet over medium heat; drain. Meanwhile, combine flour, sugar, baking powder and salt; make a well in the center. In a separate bowl, whisk together egg and butter; add to well in flour mixture and stir just until moistened. Stir in sausage and cheese. Place paper muffin liners in 12 muffin tins; spray with non-stick vegetable spray. Spoon batter into cups, filling 2/3 full. Bake at 375 degrees for 20 minutes, or until golden. Immediately remove muffins from tins. Muffins freeze well. Makes one dozen.

Grab & Go Breakfasts

Maple Breakfast Bundles

Rachel Kowasic
Valrico, FL

A quick and delicious all-in-one breakfast!

12-oz. tube refrigerated biscuits
2 to 4 T. pure maple syrup
5 slices American cheese, halved

5 brown & serve breakfast
  sausage patties, prepared
  and halved

On a floured surface, roll out biscuits into 8 to 10-inch circles. Spread each biscuit with maple syrup; top with a half-slice of cheese and a half-slice of sausage. Roll up into a bundle, folding in sides of biscuits over toppings. Place on an ungreased baking sheet; drizzle with additional syrup. Bake at 350 degrees for about 20 minutes, until golden. Makes 10 servings.

Sunrise Biscuit Buns

Lori Simmons
Princeville, IL

Eggs and bacon in a biscuit cup, what fun!

1 lb. bacon
1/2 c. onion, chopped
16.3-oz. tube refrigerated jumbo
  buttermilk biscuits

8 eggs
1/2 c. shredded sharp Cheddar
  cheese

In a skillet over medium heat, cook bacon until crisp. Remove bacon to paper towels and crumble, reserving one tablespoon of drippings in skillet. Add onion to skillet; cook and stir until tender, about 2 minutes. In a small bowl, mix bacon and onion; set aside. Spray 8 jumbo muffin cups with non-stick vegetable spray. Place one biscuit in each muffin cup, pressing dough 3/4 of the way up the sides. Divide bacon mixture evenly among biscuit cups. Crack an egg into each cup; top with cheese. Bake at 350 degrees for 30 to 35 minutes, until eggs are set. Serves 8.

Peanut Butter & Chocolate Baked Oatmeal

Amy Bradsher
Roxboro, NC

This baked oatmeal tastes almost like a giant oatmeal cookie! It's soft and moist, peanutty and swirled throughout with melted chocolate. We love to eat it with a fork and a big glass of milk. It keeps my family's tummies full until lunchtime.

3 c. quick-cooking oats,
   uncooked
1/4 c. brown sugar, packed
2 t. baking powder
3/4 t. salt
1 c. milk

2 eggs, beaten
2 T. butter, melted
2 t. vanilla extract
1/2 c. creamy peanut butter
1/2 c. semi-sweet chocolate
   chips

In a large bowl, stir together oats, brown sugar, baking powder and salt. Add milk, eggs, butter, vanilla and peanut butter; mix well. Fold in chocolate chips. Spread evenly in a greased 13"x9" baking pan. Bake, uncovered, at 350 degrees for 25 minutes. Serve warm. Makes 5 to 6 servings.

If kids aren't in the mood for traditional breakfast foods, let 'em be creative! A peanut butter sandwich, a slice of leftover pizza or a helping of last night's taco casserole will get their day off to a good start too. Add a glass of milk or fruit juice for a more balanced meal.

Grab & Go *Breakfasts*

Pumpkin Pie Baked Oatmeal

Karol Cannon
Sharpsville, IN

This oatmeal brings back special memories of eating oatmeal as a child! Good warm out of the oven..it's even good cold. Enjoy!

15-oz. can pumpkin
1/3 c. brown sugar, packed
1/3 c. egg whites, beaten
1-1/2 t. pumpkin pie spice
3/4 t. baking powder

1/4 t. salt
1-1/2 c. milk
2 c. steel-cut oats, uncooked
Optional: whipped topping or
    vanilla ice cream

In a bowl, whisk together pumpkin, brown sugar, egg whites, spice, baking powder and salt. Add milk; stir until well mixed. Stir in oats; spread in a greased 9"x9" baking pan. Cover with aluminum foil. Bake at 350 degrees for 30 minutes. Uncover; bake an additional 15 minutes. Serve warm, garnished as desired. Makes 9 servings.

Mom's Simple Baked Oatmeal

Jill Daghfal
Sugar Grove, IL

Growing up, it was always a treat when Mom made this for breakfast. My dad and all five of us kids loved it. Now I make it for my husband and three children...they love it as well!

1/3 c. butter, melted
1-1/4 c. brown sugar, packed
3 eggs, beaten
1-1/2 c. milk

3-3/4 c. quick-cooking oats,
    uncooked
2-1/2 t. baking powder

Combine all ingredients in a bowl; mix well. Spread in a greased 13"x9" baking pan. Bake at 350 degrees for 30 minutes. Makes 6 to 8 servings.

A fresh treat that's good any time of day...fruit kabobs! Just slide pineapple chunks, apple slices, grapes, orange wedges and strawberries onto a wooden skewer.

15

Melanie's Oven Omelet

Mel Chencharick
Julian, PA

Tired of standing over the stove making omelets? With this recipe you can put everything in the oven, and in 25 minutes everyone sits down at the table together...even Mom! We like ham & cheese, but you can make it any way your family likes. Try it with crispy bacon, or spice it up with 1/4 cup salsa. Give it your personal touch!

8 eggs, beaten
1/2 c. half-and-half
1 c. shredded Cheddar cheese
1 c. cooked ham, finely chopped

1/4 c. green pepper, finely
   chopped
1/4 c. onion, finely chopped

In a bowl, whisk together eggs and half-and-half until light. Stir in remaining ingredients; pour into a greased 9"x9" baking pan. Bake at 400 degrees for 25 minutes, or until set and golden. Serves 6.

Bake a family-favorite omelet or quiche in muffin cups
for individual servings in a jiffy. When making minis,
reduce the baking time by about 10 minutes,
and test for doneness with a toothpick.

Grab & Go *Breakfasts*

Country Skillet Breakfast

Judy Pittenger
Richfield, WI

A skilletful of hearty homestyle goodness. Just add some toast and jam, and your day is off to a great start!

6 slices bacon
4 c. potatoes, peeled, cooked
   and cubed
1/2 c. green pepper, chopped
2 T. onion, chopped

salt and pepper to taste
6 eggs
1 c. shredded sharp Cheddar
   cheese

Cook bacon in a skillet over medium heat until crisp. Remove bacon to a paper towel; pour off part of drippings. Add potatoes, green pepper and onion to drippings in skillet; cook until lightly golden. Season with salt and pepper. Break eggs over potato mixture. Cover and cook eggs to desired doneness. Sprinkle with cheese and crumbled bacon. Cover and let stand until cheese melts, about 5 minutes. Serves 6.

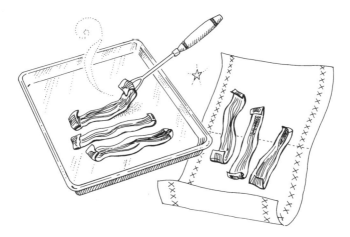

To prepare lots of crispy bacon easily, try baking it
in the oven! Place bacon slices on a broiler pan, place the
pan in a cool oven and turn the temperature to 400 degrees.

Linda's Easy Cinnamon Buns
Linda Kelly
L'Amable, Ontario

I first learned to make this recipe when I was 15 years old. It has become a standard request whenever I have family visiting. It's easy to prepare while the first pot of coffee is brewing.

2 c. all-purpose flour
2 T. sugar
4 t. baking powder
1/4 t. salt
1/4 c. plus 1/3 c. chilled butter,
   divided

1 c. milk
1 c. brown sugar, packed
1 T. cinnamon

Mix flour, sugar, baking powder and salt in a bowl. Add 1/4 cup butter and cut into flour mixture with a pastry cutter or fork. Stir in milk. On a floured surface, knead dough 9 times. Roll out to a 12-inch by 9-inch rectangle. In a separate bowl, blend together brown sugar, cinnamon and remaining butter. Drop 1/2 teaspoon brown sugar mixture into each of 12 greased muffin cups; set aside. Spread remaining brown sugar mixture evenly over dough. Carefully roll up dough jelly-roll style, starting on one long edge; cut into 12 equal slices. Place slices cut-side down into muffin cups. Bake at 350 degrees for 20 to 30 minutes. Immediately turn out buns upside-down onto a serving plate. Makes one dozen.

Cleaning your house while your kids are still growing up
is like shoveling the walk before it stops snowing.

–Phyllis Diller

Grab & Go *Breakfasts*

French Breakfast Puffs

Molly Estep
Bergton, VA

This was one of my first recipes I ever learned to make in home economics class. It was a hit with my classmates then, and it's always a hit with my family now!

1/3 c. plus 6 T. butter, softened
   and divided
1 c. sugar, divided
1 egg, beaten
1-1/2 c. all-purpose flour

1-1/2 t. baking powder
1/2 t. salt
1/4 t. nutmeg
1/2 c. milk
1 t. cinnamon

In a bowl, blend together 1/3 cup butter, 1/2 cup sugar and egg; set aside. In a separate bowl, mix together flour, baking powder, salt and nutmeg. Stir flour mixture into butter mixture alternately with milk. Spoon batter into 12 greased muffin cups, filling 2/3 full. Bake at 350 degrees for 20 to 25 minutes. Meanwhile, melt remaining butter in a cup; mix cinnamon and remaining sugar in a separate cup. While muffins are still hot, dip tops into melted butter, then dip into cinnamon-sugar. Makes one dozen.

Kids are sure to giggle when you serve up silly pancake animals! Simply put batter into a plastic zipping bag, snip off a corner and squeeze batter into a greased, hot skillet or griddle in fun shapes.

Mom's Best Granola Cereal

Kristin Price
Croton, OH

The store-bought kind can't beat this homemade granola!

1/2 c. honey
1/2 c. oil
1/2 t. vanilla extract
6 c. quick-cooking oats, uncooked
1 c. wheat germ
1 c. raisins
1/2 c. sweetened dried cranberries
1/2 c. chopped pecans or walnuts
1/2 c. unsalted sunflower kernels
1/2 c. flaked coconut

Heat together honey, oil and vanilla; set aside. Combine remaining ingredients in a large bowl. Pour honey mixture over oat mixture; stir until well coated. Spread in a greased large shallow baking pan. Bake at 300 degrees for 15 minutes, stirring after 8 minutes. Watch closely so that ingredients do not get too dark. Cool; store in a covered container. Makes 10 cups.

Cottage Cheese & Fruit Crunch

Jill Ball
Highland, UT

Mornings at our house are wild! Trying to get four kids off to school and my husband and myself off to work is crazy. I am always looking for healthy, quick breakfast ideas...this one is a winner.

1/2 c. blueberries, raspberries or strawberries
1/2 c. low-fat cottage cheese
1 banana, sliced
1/2 c. granola cereal
Optional: raisins

Divide berries between 2 bowls or parfait glasses. Layer with cottage cheese and banana; top with cereal and raisins, if desired. Serves 2.

Add the nutty taste of whole grains to breakfast...they're delicious and healthy too! Try toasted whole-wheat bread, multigrain English muffins and pancakes with a sprinkle of wheat germ stirred into the batter.

Grab & Go Breakfasts

Late-for-the-Bus Smoothies

Leslie McCullough
Liberty Twp., OH

My sons Cooper and Clay always enjoyed drinking this fruity smoothie on their walks to the bus stop.

1 c. milk
1/2 c. vanilla yogurt
1/2 c. favorite fruit juice, chilled

2 c. favorite fruit, sliced, frozen and divided
1 banana, sliced

In a blender, combine milk, yogurt, juice and half the frozen fruit; process until smooth. Add remaining frozen fruit and banana; process until smooth. Add a little more milk or juice if a thinner consistency is desired. Pour into cups with lids. Serves 3.

Pineapple-Orange Smoothies

Jennifer Hathcock
Temple, GA

This refreshing smoothie is my favorite because the fruits complement each other so well. It's so creamy and has just the right amount of sweetness...even my boys will drink it up!

1/4 c. crushed pineapple
1 clementine or 1/2 to 1 orange, peeled
1 banana, sliced and frozen

6-oz. container vanilla or plain yogurt
Garnish: orange slice, whipped cream

Combine fruits and yogurt in a blender. Process to desired consistency, adding a little milk for a thinner consistency. Pour into one to 2 glasses. Garnish as desired. Serves one to 2.

Fruit-filled smoothies are delicious and good for you! They're perfect for kids who don't have much appetite when they get up in the morning.

Fruit & Cheese Panini

Cynthia Johnson
Verona, WI

Sweet grilled cheese for breakfast...try all your favorite flavors of fruit preserves!

4 slices Italian or sourdough
    bread
1/4 c. cherry preserves

1/4 c. cream cheese, softened
2 T. butter

Spread 2 slices of bread with preserves; spread remaining slices with cream cheese. Assemble into 2 sandwiches. Preheat a non-stick skillet or panini press over medium heat. Melt butter in pan; add sandwiches to pan. Grill on both sides until golden. Slice each sandwich in half. Serves 2 to 4.

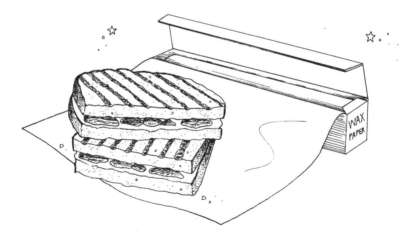

Take 'em along! Roll up a Fruit & Cheese Panini in wax paper, plastic wrap or aluminum foil, and it's ready for carrying along to school or work.

Grab & Go *Breakfasts*

Banana Bread French Toast
Paulette Alexander
Saint George's, Newfoundland

I make this often whenever our family has a get-together. Once it's cooked, you can pop it in the oven to keep warm. It also freezes well, and is great for school mornings. Just thaw a slice and warm it in the toaster or microwave...an instant yummy breakfast!

2 eggs, beaten
1/4 c. milk
1 t. honey

1 t. cinnamon
4 slices banana bread
2 to 3 T. butter

In a shallow dish, beat together eggs, milk, honey and cinnamon. Dip bread into egg mixture, coating both sides. Melt butter in a skillet over medium heat; add bread. Cook on both sides until golden. Makes 4 servings.

Cinnamon French Toast
Gloria Kaufmann
Orrville, OH

Cinnamon and vanilla add wonderful flavor to this basic French toast recipe.

2 eggs, beaten
1/2 c. milk
1/4 t. vanilla extract
1/4 t. cinnamon

1/2 t. salt
6 slices day-old bread
2 to 3 T. butter

Whisk together eggs, milk, vanilla, cinnamon and salt in a shallow dish. Dip bread into egg mixture, coating both sides. Melt butter in a skillet over medium heat; add bread and cook on both sides until golden. Makes 6 servings.

Set aside day-old bread for making French toast...
it absorbs milk better than bakery-fresh bread.

Maria's Oven Apple Pancake

Maria Kuhns
Crofton, MD

I make this dish for my children on cold winter mornings. A wonderful delight of puffy pancake, apples and maple syrup, it will warm you inside and out!

2 cooking apples, peeled, cored
   and sliced
2 T. pure maple syrup
1 T. lemon juice
4 T. butter
3 eggs, beaten

1/2 c. milk or light cream
1/2 c. all-purpose flour
1/2 t. cinnamon
1/4 t. salt
Garnish: warmed maple syrup

In a bowl, toss apples with maple syrup and lemon juice; set aside. Melt butter in a medium cast-iron skillet; remove from heat. In a separate bowl, beat eggs and milk or cream with one tablespoon melted butter. In another bowl, combine flour, cinnamon and salt; whisk into egg mixture until smooth. Return skillet to high heat; add apple mixture and sauté in remaining butter for 2 to 3 minutes. Spread apples evenly in the skillet and slowly pour in the batter. Bake at 425 degrees for 15 to 18 minutes, until very puffy and lightly golden. Cut into wedges. Serve hot or warm, drizzled with maple syrup. Serves 4 to 6.

Keep hard-boiled eggs on hand for speedy breakfast snacks. Here's a helpful tip...if you use eggs that have been refrigerated at least 7 to 10 days, the shells will slip right off.

Grab & Go *Breakfasts*

Whole-Wheat Banana Muffins

*Kim Hartless
Forest, VA*

*This is a healthy snack my children love any time of day. Sometimes
I'll use a diced apple instead of a banana...it's tasty too!*

1-1/2 c. whole-wheat flour
1/2 c. sugar
1/4 c. milled flax seed
1-1/2 t. baking powder
1/2 t. baking soda
1/2 t. salt
1 egg, beaten

1/2 c. milk
1/4 c. applesauce
1 ripe banana, mashed
1/4 c. carrot, peeled and
   shredded
1/2 c. chopped nuts

In a bowl, mix flour, sugar, flax seed, baking powder, baking soda and
salt. In a separate bowl, whisk together eggs, milk and applesauce.
Add flour mixture to egg mixture; stir well. Fold in banana, carrot and
nuts. Fill 12 greased or paper-lined muffin cups 2/3 full. Bake at
400 degrees for 18 to 20 minutes Makes one dozen.

How about setting up a cereal station for breakfast?
Pitchers of icy-cold milk paired with a variety of cereals
and fruit are tasty. You can even have packets of
instant oatmeal on hand.

Speedy Salsa-Egg Roll-Up

Pam Massey
Marshall, AR

Planning ahead makes for a simple on-the-go breakfast...saves time and money! No more drive-through breakfasts. Change it up to your taste with diced tomatoes instead of salsa, or add a few crumbles of sausage.

1 T. butter	salt and pepper to taste
2 T. salsa	8-inch flour tortilla
2 eggs, beaten	2 T. shredded Mexican cheese
2 T. bacon bits	

Melt butter in a small skillet over medium-high heat. Add salsa and heat until bubbly; pour in eggs and stir. Add bacon bits, salt and pepper; cook until eggs are set, about 2 minutes. Place tortilla on a piece of aluminum foil; top with cheese and egg mixture. Roll up tortilla and wrap in foil to take with you. Serves one.

Grab & Go Breakfast Roll-Ups

Teresa Eller
Tonganoxie, KS

If you are running a tad late at breakfast, just pop this in the microwave and eat it on the run. A great after-school snack as well.

12 slices bacon	1 T. butter
6 eggs, beaten	6 8-inch flour tortillas, warmed
1/2 c. milk	6 slices American cheese
1 t. garlic powder	

In a skillet over medium heat, cook bacon until crisp; drain on paper towels. Meanwhile, whisk eggs with milk and garlic powder. Heat butter in a skillet over medium-low heat; scramble eggs to desired doneness. To assemble, top each warmed tortilla with eggs, 2 slices bacon and one slice cheese. Roll up partway; fold in ends and finish rolling. Wrap each roll-up in a paper towel; tuck into a small plastic zipping bag and refrigerate. To serve, microwave for 30 to 40 seconds. Makes 6 servings.

Grab & Go Breakfasts

Ham & Cheese French Toast Sandwiches

Kathy Collins
Brookfield, CT

My family loves these sandwiches for weekend breakfasts. They're great when you are craving breakfast foods for dinner too.

4 eggs, beaten
2/3 c. half-and-half
8 slices bread
2 T. butter, softened

3 to 4 T. honey mustard
4 slices American cheese
4 slices deli ham

In a shallow dish, whisk together eggs and half-and-half; set aside. Spread one side of each bread slice with butter and mustard. Top 4 slices with cheese and ham; top with remaining slices. Dip each sandwich into egg mixture; let excess drip off. Place sandwiches in a preheated skillet that has been lightly coated with non-stick vegetable spray. Cook on each side for 3 minutes, or until golden and cheese melts. Serves 4.

Fruity breakfast roll-ups are sure to be a hit...ready to eat in a snap! Spread a whole-grain tortilla with low-fat cream cheese, and top with sliced strawberries. Roll up tight and slice into pinwheels.

Crystal's Best Granola Bars

Crystal Shook
Catawba, NC

These make a great breakfast on the run or after-school snack.

2-1/2 c. crispy rice cereal
2-1/2 c. quick-cooking oats,
   uncooked
1/4 c. sweetened dried
   cranberries
1/4 c. raisins

1/4 c. candy-coated chocolates
1/4 c. peanuts
1/2 c. brown sugar, packed
1/2 c. light corn syrup
1/2 c. creamy peanut butter
1 t. vanilla extract

Combine cereal, oats, cranberries, raisins, chocolates and peanuts in a large heat-proof bowl; set aside. In a saucepan over medium heat, bring brown sugar and corn syrup to a boil. Remove from heat; stir in peanut butter and vanilla. Pour over cereal mixture; stir to combine and press into a lightly greased 13"x9" baking pan. Cool; cut into bars. Makes one dozen.

Save bottom-of-the-box leftovers of crunchy
breakfast cereal in a canister to use in a favorite recipe.
Homemade cereal bars will be just as tasty...
and you'll be saving money!

On-the-Go Breakfast Parfait

Kim Wilson
Melbourne, FL

*This parfait can be prepared the day before and then it's ready
in the morning when you need it. If you're making it a day ahead,
toss the apple with a little lemon juice to prevent darkening.*

1/4 c. fresh or frozen raspberries	1/2 c. vanilla yogurt
1/3 c. chopped walnuts	1/3 c. granola cereal
1 apple, peeled, cored and diced	

In a container with a lid, layer ingredients in the order given. Cover
and refrigerate until ready to eat. Stir up ingredients just before
serving. Makes one serving.

Hang some pegs near inside the back door so everyone knows
just where to find their coat or sweater, backpack and other
must-have items every morning.

Sunshine State Smoothies

Julie Dossantos
Fort Pierce, FL

This smoothie combines the citrus goodness from our home state of Florida with other healthful fruits and veggies.

4 to 5 ice cubes
1 peach, halved, pitted and
   cubed
4-oz. container low-fat peach
   or vanilla yogurt

1 to 2 bananas, sliced
1/4 c. orange juice
10 baby carrots
Optional: orange or peach slices

Combine all ingredients except optional garnish in a blender. Process well for about one minute. Pour into 2 glasses; garnish with fruit slices, if desired. Serves 2.

California Dream Smoothies

Sonya Labbe
West Hollywood, CA

This is what California is all about...sunshine and dreams. A delicious creamy drink. Kids love it too!

6-oz. can frozen orange juice
   concentrate
1 c. milk
1/2 c. half-and-half

1/4 c. powdered sugar
1 t. vanilla extract
1-1/2 c. ice cubes

In a blender, combine all ingredients. Process until smooth. Divide into 4 glasses. Makes 4 servings.

Using frozen fruit in smoothies will make them icy-cold without adding extra water from ice cubes.

Brown-
BAGGING IT

Ham-It-Up Salad Wraps

Carole Weaver
Marietta, GA

My kids love these wraps for lunch and snacks. Sliced in half, the wraps are also a welcome addition to party trays.

8 slices deli ham
8 6-inch flour tortillas
1 c. fresh spinach, torn
2 c. romaine lettuce, torn
1 c. tomatoes, diced
1 c. cucumber, diced
1 c. shredded Cheddar cheese
1/2 c. bacon bits
ranch salad dressing to taste

Place one ham slice on each tortilla. Layer with remaining ingredients, adding salad dressing to taste. Fold in 2 sides of each tortilla; roll up burrito-style. For a pretty presentation, slice in half at an angle. Makes 8 servings.

Hawaiian Pinwheels

Cynthia Johnson
Verona, WI

Easy and yummy for lunch bags or after-school snacks!

4 6-inch whole-wheat or
    spinach tortillas
1/4 c. pineapple cream cheese
    spread
12 slices deli ham
4 slices Colby Jack cheese
1 c. romaine lettuce, shredded

Place tortillas on a microwave-safe plate; microwave for 30 seconds. Spread each tortilla with one tablespoon cream cheese; top each with 3 slices of ham, one cheese slice and 1/4 cup lettuce. Roll up tortillas; slice into one-inch pinwheels. Serves 4 to 6.

Make a healthy light wrap for smaller appetites...place sandwich toppings on lettuce leaves instead of tortillas and roll up.

Brown-Bagging It

Tuna Egg Salad

Lisa Ann Panzino DiNunzio
Vineland, NJ

This sandwich combines two popular fillings, tuna salad and egg salad...the result is positively scrumptious! Serve it spooned into pita rounds or crusty rolls, as a salad in scooped-out tomatoes or simply on a bed of lettuce.

2 5-oz. cans water-packed albacore tuna, drained and flaked
3 eggs, hard-boiled, peeled and chopped

1 T. onion, finely chopped
1 T. celery, finely chopped
6 to 8 T. olive oil mayonnaise
salt and pepper to taste
Optional: 2 t. mustard

Combine all ingredients in a bowl. Mix until well blended. Serve as desired. Makes 4 servings.

Freeze juice boxes or mini water bottles to tuck into lunches. They'll keep the whole lunch cool...and by lunchtime, the beverage will be thawed and ready to enjoy. As a bonus, your child won't have to bring home a reusable ice pack.

Brian's Salad Wraps

Janet Sharp
Milford, OH

A tasty, healthy lunch! Our son Brian makes these healthy wraps for his lunch quite often, putting them in the refrigerator to chill overnight to take for his lunch the next day. They are also very good with a side of refried beans for a meatless dinner meal.

2 c. romaine lettuce, chopped
1/2 c. tomato, chopped
1/2 c. cucumber, chopped
1/2 c. green pepper, chopped
2 T. onion, chopped
1/4 t. garlic powder

1/4 t. dried basil
3 T. chipotle ranch salad
  dressing
4 8-inch spinach tortilla wraps
3/4 c. shredded Mexican-blend
  or Cheddar cheese

In a large bowl, toss lettuce with vegetables; sprinkle with garlic powder and basil. Drizzle with salad dressing; lightly toss again. Spoon 1/2 cup of mixture into the center of each wrap; top with 3 tablespoons cheese. Fold sides of wrap toward center; roll up like a burrito. For best flavor, wrap in aluminum foil and refrigerate overnight. Makes 4 servings.

Whip up a tasty dip for sliced fruit. Simply swirl
some low-sugar fruit preserves into plain Greek yogurt.
Hungry kids will love it any time of day...
easy to pack in a lunchbox too.

Brown-Bagging It

Garbanzo Garden Pitas

Jen Thomas
Santa Rosa, CA

A delicious meatless sandwich filling to whip up in a jiffy.

19-oz. can garbanzo beans,
   drained and rinsed
1 stalk celery, chopped
1/4 c. onion, chopped
1 T. lemon juice

1 t. dill weed
1 T. mayonnaise, or to taste
3 to 4 pita rounds, halved
   and split
Garnish: tomato slices

In a bowl, mash garbanzo beans with a fork until smooth. Stir in celery, onion, lemon juice and dill weed; add mayonnaise to desired consistency. Spoon into pita rounds; garnish with tomato. Makes 3 to 4 servings.

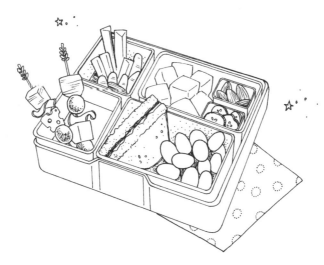

Finger foods make any packed lunch more fun! Fill the compartments of a sectioned container with a variety of your kids' favorite finger foods...cubes of deli turkey and cheese, animal crackers, baby carrots and ranch dressing. They're sure to help you think of plenty more!

Leona's Apple-Carrot Slaw

Leona Krivda
Belle Vernon, PA

A sweet slaw that's a little different...full of healthy ingredients that kids are sure to love! Sometimes I also add a large handful of broccoli slaw mix.

1/2 c. sweetened dried
    cranberries
1/2 c. orange juice, divided
2 Granny Smith apples, cored
    and cut into matchsticks
4 carrots, peeled and cut into
    matchsticks

1/4 c. red onion, thinly sliced
1/2 c. pumpkin seed kernels
1/4 c. chopped pecans
3 T. olive oil
pepper to taste

Combine cranberries and 1/4 cup orange juice in a small bowl; set aside. In a separate bowl, toss apples with remaining orange juice; add carrots, onion, pumpkin seeds and pecans. Drain cranberries, reserving the orange juice; add cranberries to apple mixture. Whisk reserved orange juice with olive oil; pour over salad. Season with pepper; toss lightly to coat well. Serve chilled or at room temperature. Makes 4 servings.

Paper napkins are a must in any packed lunch...
they're sure to brighten someone's day, too! Stock up on
festive party napkins when on sale, or let kids decorate
plain napkins with stickers and rubber stamps.

Brown-Bagging It

Goldilocks's Salad

Jill Ball
Highland, UT

*I'm not sure where this name came from...but one day
my kids started calling it Goldilocks's Salad and it stuck!
Now we all enjoy this easy-to-make salad.*

1 head cauliflower, cut into
   bite-size pieces
6 slices bacon, cooked and
   crumbled
1/4 c. red onion, diced

1/2 c. mayonnaise
1 c. ranch salad dressing
1/4 c. sugar
1/2 c. grated Parmesan cheese

Combine cauliflower, bacon and onion in a large bowl; set aside.
Combine remaining ingredients in a separate bowl; stir well. Add
mayonnaise mixture to cauliflower mixture just before serving; toss to
mix well. Keep chilled. Makes 8 servings.

Kids are more likely to eat salads if vegetables are cut into
bite-size pieces that can easily be eaten with a fork or spoon. A
mix of crunchy textures (never soggy!) and bright colors is
sure to appeal to young appetites.

Turkey BLT Roll-Ups

Jewel Sharpe
Raleigh, NC

Yum...who wouldn't love these hearty, satisfying roll-ups?

1/4 c. chive & onion cream
   cheese spread
2 T. mayonnaise
8 slices bacon, diced and crisply
   cooked

4 8-inch flour tortillas
6-oz. pkg. thinly sliced deli
   turkey
1 c. roma tomatoes, chopped
1 c. lettuce, shredded

In a small bowl, mix cream cheese and mayonnaise; stir in bacon.
Spread cream cheese mixture over each tortilla. Top with turkey,
tomatoes and lettuce; roll tortillas up tightly. Serve immediately, or
wrap in plastic wrap and refrigerate up to 24 hours. Serves 4.

Mashed Potato Salad

Sandy Pittman
Granby, MO

We used to have this potato salad when I was a girl at home.
It's loved and requested by family & friends alike...a quick and
delicious way to use up leftover mashed potatoes.

4 c. cold mashed potatoes
3/4 c. mayonnaise-style salad
   dressing
1/3 c. mustard

1/2 c. onion, diced
4 to 5 dill pickles, diced
5 eggs, hard-boiled, peeled
   and chopped

Place mashed potatoes in a large bowl. Add salad dressing and
mustard; stir together. Stir in onion and pickles; gently fold in eggs.
Cover and chill until serving time. Serves 6 to 8.

My mother had a great deal of trouble with me,
but I think she enjoyed it.

–Mark Twain

Brown-Bagging It

Buffalo Chicken Roll-Ups

Deanne Birkestrand
Minden, NE

These roll-ups pack well in lunches...they're delicious
and satisfying with a side of fresh fruit.

6-oz. pkg. frozen grilled chicken
   breast strips
3/8 t. hot pepper sauce,
   or to taste
2 8-inch whole-wheat tortillas

1/4 c. ranch salad dressing,
   or to taste
2 c. fresh baby spinach
1/4 c. shredded Parmesan
   cheese

Place frozen chicken strips in a microwave-safe bowl. Microwave for one to 2 minutes, until heated through. Drain and add hot sauce, stirring well to coat. Spread tortillas with salad dressing and cover with spinach leaves. Place chicken strips in a row, down the center of tortillas; sprinkle with cheese. Fold in both sides of each tortilla. Roll up tightly, placing seam-side down. Slice in half for easier handling. Serve immediately, or wrap in plastic wrap. Serves 2.

Encourage kids to try fruits & veggies in a rainbow
of colors. Let them choose a different one whenever they go
with you to the farmers' market or grocery store,
then taste it prepared in different ways. They're sure
to find some new favorites!

Tomato-Brown Rice Soup

Misty Nagel
Virginia Beach, VA

*This soup is surprisingly satisfying despite its humble ingredients...
my whole family loves it. The recipe comes from my Grandma Ann,
who often made it for her four children years ago. The recipe makes
plenty, so you can pack leftovers in lunchboxes the next day.*

10 c. water, divided
3/4 c. long-cooking brown rice,
    uncooked
1/2 to 1 lb. ground beef
salt and pepper to taste

3 14-oz. cans tomato sauce
4 stalks celery, diced
1/2 c. red onion, diced
2 T. beef soup base

In a large soup pot over medium-high heat, bring 4 cups water to
a boil; stir in rice. Cover and cook for 20 minutes; do not drain.
Meanwhile, in a skillet over medium heat, brown beef. Season beef
with salt and pepper; drain and set aside. After rice has cooked for
20 minutes, stir in remaining water, tomato sauce, celery, onion and
soup base; bring to a boil. Add beef; reduce heat to medium-low.
Cover and simmer for 30 minutes. Season with more salt and pepper
as desired. Add more water as necessary when reheating. Makes
10 servings.

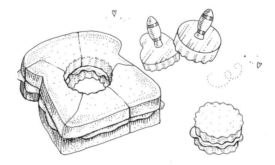

Delight finicky eaters with jigsaw puzzle sandwiches. Press a
cookie cutter straight down in the center of a sandwich, then
slice the outer part of sandwich into 3 or 4 pieces. It works
great with grilled cheese or peanut butter & jelly!

Brown-Bagging It

Vegetable Soup in a Jar

Theresa Manley
Conshohocken, PA

When I was in my senior year of high school, my grandmother shared this recipe with me not long before she passed away. She sometimes made this quick version of her homemade vegetable soup for my grandfather's, aunts' & uncles' lunches.

1-pt. wide-mouthed canning jar
  with lid
1/2 c. capellini or angel hair
  pasta, uncooked and broken
  into short pieces
1 env. instant vegetable or
  chicken broth
1/4 t. dried basil and/or parsley
1 carrot, peeled and thinly sliced
1/2 c. fresh spinach or Swiss
  chard, torn
1/4 t. garlic, minced
1 to 1-1/2 c. hot water

In the jar, layer all ingredients except water in the order listed. Add lid; use within a few hours. To serve, add desired amount of hot water to jar. Cover and let stand for 10 to 15 minutes. Serves one.

Freshen up a thermos or sports bottle in a jiffy. Spoon in a heaping teaspoon of baking soda, then fill with boiling water. Cap, shake gently and rinse...all ready to use again!

Sesame Chicken Tea Sandwiches

Jenn Erickson
Pacific Grove, CA

These elegant little tea sandwiches are a wonderful addition to a classic tea party, shower or brunch, and even to your child's lunchbox. My daughters Maddie and Mackenzie love them! It's a wonderful way to use leftover chicken.

3 c. cooked chicken, finely
   chopped
1 c. light mayonnaise, divided
1/4 c. celery, inner stalk and
   leaves, minced
2 t. sesame oil

1/4 c. sliced almonds
salt and pepper to taste
20 slices soft whole-wheat
   sandwich bread
1/2 c. toasted sesame seed

In a bowl, combine chicken, 3/4 cup mayonnaise, celery and sesame oil. Crush almonds in your palm and add to bowl; stir to mix. Season with salt and pepper. For each sandwich, place a small scoop of chicken salad on a slice of bread. Top with another slice of bread; press lightly and trim crusts. Cut into 4 triangles on the diagonal. Using a butter knife, spread a thin layer of remaining mayonnaise along the sides of each tea sandwich; dip sandwich into sesame seed to coat mayonnaise. Makes 40 mini sandwiches.

Packed lunches needn't be the same ol' sandwich...leftovers from dinnertime favorites will be anticipated eagerly by kids. Why not wrap up chicken drumsticks, quesadillas or burritos to go, or fill a mini thermos with hot mac & cheese?

Brown-Bagging It

Tiffany's Twisted Egg Salad

Tiffany Jones
Locust Grove, AR

As a teacher, I am always trying to find fun things to take for lunch. I like egg salad but wanted something with a different twist. This recipe is what I came up with! It's yummy on sliced bread, crackers or salad greens.

8 eggs, hard-boiled, peeled and
    halved
1/4 c. ranch salad dressing

1/4 c. bacon bits
1/4 c. dill pickles, diced

Separate egg whites and yolks; reserve yolks for another use. Chop egg whites; combine with remaining ingredients and stir gently. Cover and chill if not serving immediately. Makes 8 servings.

Mamaw's Special Tuna Salad

Tina Butler
Royse City, TX

My husband grew up on tuna salad with a bit of apple in the recipe. It really does make the sandwich...this is a favorite at our house!

5-oz. can tuna, drained
    and flaked
5 to 6 T. mayonnaise
1 Granny Smith apple, peeled,
    cored and shredded

2 T. pickle relish
salt and pepper to taste
bread slices, croissants,
    crackers or pita rounds
Optional: lettuce

In a bowl, lightly stir together tuna, mayonnaise, apple and relish; season with salt and pepper. Serve on bread or croissants lined with lettuce, spread on crackers or stuffed in pita pockets. Serves 2.

It doesn't take much to say "I love you" in a lunchbox... just a little note or even a silly joke will do the trick.

Crispy Pita Pizza

Sally Kelly
Akron, OH

*Our kids love this pizza in their lunches! It's easy to make it special
with their favorite toppings too. I cut it in quarters and place in a
sandwich-size plastic zipping bag for easy packing.*

1 whole pita round
2 to 3 T. pizza sauce
2 to 3 T. shredded mozzarella
   cheese

8 to 10 pepperoni slices
Optional: additional favorite
   toppings

Spread uncut pita with desired amount of pizza sauce. Add cheese,
pepperoni and other toppings, as desired. Place on an ungreased
baking sheet. Bake at 400 degrees for 11 minutes, or until cheese is
melted. Cut into wedges. Makes one serving.

Creamy Veggie Sandwiches

Kelly Alderson
Erie, PA

*My kids like this meatless sandwich spread very much. Sometimes
we'll change it up by adding diced cucumber, thinly sliced radish
or whatever else is on hand in the fridge.*

1/4 c. broccoli flowerets
1/4 c. red pepper, diced
1/2 c. carrot, peeled and finely
   shredded

1-1/4 c. ricotta cheese
4 slices whole-wheat or country-
   style bread, crusts trimmed

Place broccoli in a small microwave-safe bowl; add one tablespoon
water. Cover with plastic wrap. Microwave for 3 minutes, or until
crisp-tender. Drain well and cool; chop finely. In a separate bowl,
combine broccoli, remaining vegetables and ricotta cheese. Spread
mixture on 2 slices bread; top with remaining bread. Serves 2.

Pita halves are perfect for all kinds of sandwich fillings...
extra easy for little hands to hold without spills.

Brown-Bagging It

Ham & Cheese Pockets

Kristin Pittis
Dennison, OH

Frozen dinner rolls make these sandwiches quick & easy. I like to put the frozen rolls out to thaw and rise before leaving for work and they're ready when I get home. A mixture of Cheddar and Swiss cheese is delicious too.

12 frozen dinner rolls
1 c. cooked ham, diced

1 c. shredded Cheddar cheese

Thaw rolls according to package instructions. Flatten each thawed dinner roll into a 4-inch circle. Top rolls with 1-1/2 tablespoons ham and 1-1/2 tablespoons cheese each. Place remaining rolls on top; pinch edges to seal. Place pockets on a baking sheet sprayed with non-stick vegetable spray. Bake at 350 degrees for 15 minutes, or until golden. Makes 6 servings.

Serve up an old favorite, ants on a log...celery sticks filled with peanut butter and sprinkled with raisins. Or substitute dried cranberries to make fire ants on a log, just for fun!

45

Spicy Chicken Wraps

Pam Massey
Marshall, AR

These wraps make a simple, flavorful lunch that's really low in fat and calories.

5-oz. can chicken breast, drained and flaked
1 T. pico de gallo
1 t. low-fat mayonnaise or salad dressing

2 sweet pickles, chopped
2 8-inch flour tortillas, warmed
Garnish: sour cream, shredded lettuce

In a bowl, combine chicken, pico de gallo, mayonnaise or salad dressing and pickles. Spread tortillas with a little sour cream and sprinkle with lettuce; top with chicken mixture. Roll up tortillas burrito-style. Makes 2 servings.

Easy Caprese Salad

Peggy Donnally
Toledo, OH

This tasty twist on a classic salad stores well in the fridge. It's a perfect portable for brown bag lunches and picnics.

3 English cucumbers, peeled and diced
2 t. dried basil
2 pts. grape tomatoes, sliced

12 pieces string cheese, sliced
pepper to taste
Optional: balsamic vinegar

In a bowl, toss cucumbers with basil. Add tomatoes and cheese; toss gently and season generously with pepper. Serve plain or with a spritz of balsamic vinegar. Makes 6 to 8 servings.

Tired of sandwiches? Turn 'em inside-out! Wrap thin slices of deli meat and cheese around crunchy rod pretzels or soft bread sticks.

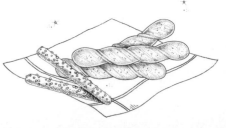

Brown-Bagging It

Chicken-Bacon Sandwich Spread

Rosalind Dickinson
Grandview, WA

This makes a delicious and healthy sandwich...kids love it! Spread it on crackers for an appetizer or spoon it onto crisp romaine lettuce for a salad. Sometimes I'll change up the cheese...Pepper Jack is great for adding a little zip and blue cheese crumbles are tasty too.

2 boneless, skinless chicken breasts, cooked and diced or shredded
1/3 c. bacon, crisply cooked and crumbled, or bacon bits
1/4 c. sweet onion, finely chopped
2/3 c. light mayonnaise-type salad dressing
salt-free herb seasoning to taste
8 to 10 slices multi-grain bread
Optional: 4 to 6 cheese slices, romaine lettuce

In a bowl, combine chicken, bacon, onion and 1/3 cup salad dressing. Stir; add remaining dressing to desired consistency. More dressing may be added to make a spread for crackers. Season to taste with herb seasoning. To serve, spread chicken mixture on bread; add cheese and lettuce, if desired. Serves 4 to 5.

Make your own baked tortilla chips...it's easy. Spritz both sides of corn or flour tortillas with non-stick vegetable spray. Cut into wedges and microwave on high setting for 5 to 6 minutes, turning wedges over every 1-1/2 minutes. Sprinkle warm chips with salt and serve.

Creamy Chicken-Cheese Soup
Denise Pendleton
Chino Hills, CA

My kids especially love this soup...mostly because they get to add a spoonful of shredded cheese on top!

1/4 onion, chopped
3 T. butter
1/3 c. all-purpose flour
2 c. milk
10-1/2 oz. can chicken broth
1 t. Worcestershire sauce
1/4 t. pepper
12-1/2 oz. can chunk chicken
   breast, drained and flaked
1 c. shredded Cheddar cheese,
   divided

In a saucepan over medium-low heat, cook onion in butter for 8 to 10 minutes, until tender and golden. Stir in flour. Slowly add milk, broth, sauce and pepper. Cook and stir until thickened and bubbly. Stir in chicken and 1/2 cup cheese. Cook and stir over low heat until cheese melts. Top each bowl with a spoonful of remaining cheese. Makes 4 servings.

A toasty touch for soups! Butter bread slices and cut into shapes using mini cookie cutters. Place on a baking sheet and bake at 425 degrees until crisp.

Brown-Bagging It

Babies' Beef & Noodle Soup

Jessica Minor
Lawrence, KS

*Fast, easy, and a great serving of vegetables! My kids love this
and it makes enough for leftovers for lunch throughout the week.*

1 lb. ground beef
48-oz. can cocktail vegetable
   juice
1.35-oz. pkg. onion soup mix

3-oz. pkg. beef ramen noodles,
   divided
16-oz. pkg. frozen mixed
   vegetables

Brown beef in a large saucepan over medium heat; drain. Stir in juice,
soup mix, ramen seasoning packet and vegetables; bring to a boil.
Reduce heat to medium-low. Simmer, uncovered, for 6 minutes or until
vegetables are tender. Return to a boil and stir in ramen noodles; cook
for 3 minutes, until noodles are tender. Makes 8 servings.

A wide-mouthed thermos is terrific for keeping soup,
mac & cheese and other warm foods fresh and delicious. To
keep the thermos hot until lunchtime, fill it with
hot water, then empty it just before adding the
piping-hot soup or food.

Greek Salad Pitas

Lisa Ann Panzino DiNunzio
Vineland, NJ

*Simple, fresh and wholesome ingredients make these sandwiches
healthy and delicious!*

3 T. extra-virgin olive oil
1-1/2 T. cider vinegar or
　balsamic vinegar
salt and pepper to taste
1 c. tomatoes, diced
1 c. cucumber, diced

1/4 c. Kalamata olives, diced
4 to 6 romaine lettuce leaves,
　torn into bite-size pieces
1 c. crumbled feta cheese
4 to 6 whole-wheat pita rounds,
　halved and split

In a large bowl, whisk together olive oil, vinegar, salt and pepper. Add
tomatoes, cucumber, olives and lettuce; mix well. Add cheese and toss
gently. Using a slotted spoon, transfer salad into pita halves. Serves 4
to 6.

PB & J sandwiches can be made ahead of time and frozen...
make a week's worth at a time! Spread peanut butter all the
way to the edge of 2 slices of bread, then spread jam or jelly on
just one slice, stopping 1/2-inch from the edge. Press slices
together, wrap individually and freeze. Tucked in a lunchbox,
the sandwich will thaw in time for lunch.

Brown-Bagging It

Jacob's Superman Salad

Janis Parr
Campbellford, Ontario

I occasionally babysit a 4-year-old boy for a friend of mine. Jacob is very picky, so I have come up with a quick and nutritious meal for him that features foods he likes. I explained that vegetables will make him strong and healthy, so he calls it his Superman Salad.

12-oz. pkg. mixed salad greens
9-oz. can mandarin oranges,
   drained and 2 T. juice
   reserved
1 apple, peeled, cored and cubed
1 T. bacon bits

1/2 c. mini marshmallows
1 egg, hard-boiled, peeled
   and diced
Optional: favorite salad dressing
   to taste

Place salad greens in a large bowl. Add oranges and reserved orange juice; toss to combine. Add apple cubes and bacon bits; toss again. Add marshmallows and stir to combine. Sprinkle egg over top of salad. Cover and refrigerate. At serving time, drizzle with salad dressing, if desired. Makes 4 to 6 servings.

Nobody likes fruit that's turned brown! To keep just-cut fruit slices and cubes looking fresh, soak them in a little lemon juice and water before serving. Ginger ale works well too.

Peanut Butter-Honey Roll-Ups

Patti Walker
Mocksville, NC

When my children were younger, they always seemed to get the munchies when we were away from home. I came up with these little sandwiches to take along, tucked in a plastic bag. They aren't nearly as messy as a regular sandwich and kids love the fact that they are crustless. Serve with apple slices and milk.

6 slices soft white bread,   3/4 c. creamy peanut butter
   crusts trimmed   honey to taste

Using a rolling pin, roll bread slices until thin. Spread each piece of bread with 2 tablespoons of peanut butter. Drizzle honey lightly over the peanut butter. Roll each piece of bread tightly into a tube. Makes 6 servings.

Peanut Butter-Honey Bites

Jill Ball
Highland, UT

I'm always looking for easy, healthy new ideas for school lunches. My children got tired of the same old thing, so I came up with this idea...they love it!

1 c. creamy peanut butter   12 snack-size apple-cinnamon
1 c. honey   rice cakes
1 t. cinnamon

Combine peanut butter, honey and cinnamon in a large bowl. Beat with an electric mixer on medium speed until blended. Cover and keep refrigerated. To serve, spread on 6 rice cakes and top each with another rice cake. Makes 6 servings.

Brown-Bagging It

Peanut Butter & Banana Wraps
Linda Belon
Wintersville, OH

These wraps are great for breakfast or for packed lunches, nutritious and low in calories.

4 6-inch flour tortillas
1/4 c. crunchy peanut butter

3 to 4 ripe bananas, mashed
2 T. honey or maple syrup

Spread tortillas with peanut butter; top with mashed bananas and drizzle with honey or maple syrup. Roll up and slice in half. Makes 4 servings.

Grilled PB & J
Cris Goode
Mooresville, IN

My little girl Addie and I love to grill up a couple of these childhood favorites for a great comforting treat!

4 slices bread
1/4 c. creamy peanut butter

2 T. grape jelly
2 T. butter, softened

Using the bread, peanut butter and jelly, make 2 sandwiches. Spread butter lightly on the outside of each sandwich. Grill in a hot skillet over medium heat until toasted on both sides. Slice sandwiches in half. Makes 2 to 4 servings.

Looking for an alternative to peanut butter? Try sun butter, made from sunflower seeds, or soy nut butter, made from soybeans. If your child has a peanut allergy, check with his or her doctor first, to be on the safe side.

Pizza Grilled Cheese

Debbie Manning
Northlake, TX

My two boys and I love pizza as well as grilled cheese sandwiches, so I came up with the idea of combining the two. Now when I ask what they want for lunch, they tell me Pizza Grilled Cheese! It's pretty inexpensive and so quick & easy.

1 to 2 t. butter, softened
2 slices white or whole-wheat
    bread
2 slices mozzarella cheese
dried oregano to taste
grated Parmesan cheese to taste
10 to 12 mini pepperoni slices
Garnish: warmed pizza or
    marinara sauce

Spread butter over both sides of bread. Lay one slice of bread butter-side down in a non-stick skillet over medium-high heat. Top with one cheese slice; sprinkle with a little oregano and Parmesan cheese. Add pepperoni slices and remaining cheese. Top with remaining bread, butter-side up. Toast on both sides until golden and cheese is melted. Slice in half; serve with warm sauce for dipping. Makes one serving.

Chalkboard paint is a terrific way to turn practically any surface into a blackboard...how about the inside lid of your child's lunchbox? Now chalk messages or games of tic-tac-toe can easily be erased with a paper towel or napkin!

54

Brown-Bagging It

Fast Phillies

Teresa Eller
Tonganoxie, KS

I ordered a sandwich from a pizza place one night when I didn't feel like cooking. I looked at the sandwich and at the receipt and thought to myself, I can do this a lot cheaper! So here you are...it only takes a few minutes for a great sandwich. Serve with chips & dip.

1 onion, thinly sliced
1 green pepper, thinly sliced
1 c. sliced mushrooms
1 T. extra-virgin olive oil
1/2 lb. deli sliced roast beef

2 T. butter
1 T. garlic powder
4 ciabatta rolls, split
8-oz. pkg. shredded white
    pasteurized process cheese

In a skillet over medium heat, sauté onion, green pepper and mushrooms in olive oil until tender. Add beef to mixture in skillet; warm through and remove to a plate. Blend butter and garlic powder in a cup; spread over rolls. Toast rolls butter-side down in skillet. To assemble sandwiches, divide half of cheese among the bottom halves of rolls; add vegetable and beef mixture. Top with remaining cheese; add top halves of rolls. Makes 4 servings.

For a crunchy treat that kids love, nothing beats popcorn! Good for them too, because it's a whole grain. To add new flavor, sprinkle popcorn with cinnamon-sugar, taco seasoning or grated Parmesan cheese before filling snack-size plastic bags.

ABC Soup Mix in a Jar

Janet Myers
Reading, PA

I made jars of this soup mix as favors for my son & daughter-in-law's
ABC baby shower. Everyone loved them and took home
a delicious meal for a chilly day.

1/2 c. dried split peas
1/3 c. beef bouillon granules
1/4 c. pearl barley
1/2 c. dried lentils
1/4 c. dried, minced onion

2 t. Italian seasoning
1/2 c. long-cooking rice
1/2 c. alphabet pasta
1-qt. wide-mouthed Mason jar
   with lid

Layer all ingredients in jar in the order listed. Add lid; seal tightly.
Attach directions to jar. Makes one jar.

Directions:

Remove pasta from jar; set aside. In a Dutch oven, brown one pound
of ground beef or turkey; drain. Add 3 quarts water, one 28-ounce can
diced tomatoes with juice and contents of soup mix jar; bring to a boil.
Reduce heat; cover and simmer for 45 minutes. Stir in pasta; cover and
simmer for 5 to 10 minutes, until pasta is tender. Makes 4 quarts,
about 16 servings.

Quick breads make yummy lunchbox sandwiches. Top slices
of pumpkin or banana bread with peanut butter, jam, flavored
cream cheese or apple slices. Kids will love 'em!

Healthy Bites
FOR SNACKING

Veggie Dipping Cups

Janis Parr
Campbellford, Ontario

*These fresh, colorful snacks are all ready for after-school snacking.
Feel free to use whatever vegetables your kids like...fresh
mushrooms and sliced zucchini are tasty too!*

1 c. favorite creamy dip
   for vegetables
12 cherry tomatoes
2 stalks celery, cut into
   3-inch sticks

3 carrots, peeled and cut into
   3-inch sticks
1 yellow pepper, cut into
   3-inch sticks

Divide dip among 4 small clear plastic cups. Divide vegetables among
cups. Cover with plastic wrap; serve immediately or refrigerate.
Serves 4.

Make a healthy veggie dip. Combine 2/3 cup Greek yogurt,
one tablespoon olive oil and one tablespoon chopped
fresh dill...dip away!

Donna's Mango Salsa

*Donna Wilson
Maryville, TN*

My very picky kids tried this salsa and surprise...they loved how it tasted! If it can please Holly, Matthew, Stacia, Kyra and Adriana, it'll please your picky kids too.

1 mango, peeled, pitted
   and diced
1 red pepper, diced
1 to 2 jalapeño peppers, seeded
   and minced

1 red onion, diced
zest and juice of 1 lime
1/2 t. chili lime rub
1/2 t. salt
tortilla chips

Combine all ingredients except tortilla chips in a bowl; mix well. If a smoother texture is desired, transfer mixture to a blender; process to desired consistency. Serve with tortilla chips. Makes 4 to 6 servings.

Make some wonton chips for snacking. Separate refrigerated wonton wrappers and cut each in half, forming 2 triangles. Spray lightly on both sides with non-stick vegetabl e spray and arrange on a baking sheet. Bake at 350 degrees for 5 to 7 minutes, until crisp and golden. Sprinkle warm chips with salt or seasonings, if you like.

Bug Juice Smoothies

Diana Chaney
Olathe, KS

Mix & match your kids' favorite berry and yogurt flavors!

2 c. fat-free fruit-flavored or
   vanilla yogurt
2 ripe bananas, cut into chunks

1 c. frozen strawberries
1 c. orange juice

Combine all ingredients in a blender. Cover and process on high speed for about 30 seconds, until smooth. Serve immediately. Makes 4 servings.

Slimer Smoothies

Regina Wickline
Pebble Beach, CA

Sweet pears make this healthy green smoothie appealing to kids.

2 c. baby spinach
1 cucumber, peeled and cut
   into chunks

2 ripe pears, cored and cut
   into chunks
1/2 c. water

Combine all ingredients in a blender. Cover and process on medium speed for about 30 seconds, until smooth. Serve immediately. Serves 2 to 4.

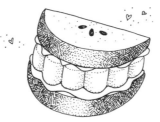

Make "apple smiles" with your little ones! Cut apples into eight wedges. Spread peanut butter on one side of each wedge. Place mini marshmallows on the peanut butter for teeth. Place another peanut-buttered apple slice on top, sandwiching the marshmallows in between.

Healthy Bites
For Snacking

Tasty Parmesan Pretzels

Pat Wissler
Harrisburg, PA

*My kids love these crunchy pretzels. They always ask for them
and the recipe is so easy to make, there's no reason not to!*

12-oz. pkg. mini twist pretzels	1/4 t. garlic powder
1/4 c. butter, sliced	1/4 c. grated Parmesan cheese

Place pretzels in a large microwave-safe bowl; set aside. Combine
butter and garlic powder in a one-cup glass measure. Microwave,
uncovered, on high for 30 to 45 seconds, until melted; stir to combine.
Drizzle butter mixture over pretzels; mix lightly. Sprinkle with cheese;
mix again. Return to microwave. Microwave on high, uncovered,
for 3 to 4 minutes; stir once or twice. Cool. Store in a tightly covered
container.

Keep your family's favorite crunchy snacks handy in
big unbreakable plastic jars, and label each jar with a
family face. Colorful photos glued on each jar will
remind snackers of what's inside.

Viva's Frozen Fruit Cups

Kathy Werner
Melbourne, FL

This recipe is delicious, refreshing and versatile. It was passed down from my husband's Great-Aunt Viva. My middle son Luke always requests it when he's home from college. The fruit cups can be served in tall glasses, with ginger ale poured over the icy fruit, or freeze the mixture in a 13"x9" baking pan and cut into squares.

20-oz. can crushed pineapple
   with juice
12-oz. can frozen orange juice
   concentrate, thawed
10-oz. pkg. frozen strawberries,
   thawed

6 ripe bananas, sliced
1-1/2 c. cold water
1/4 c. lemon juice
1 c. sugar

Combine undrained pineapple and remaining ingredients in a large bowl; stir until sugar dissolves. Ladle into twelve 9-ounce plastic punch cups; cover and freeze. Remove from freezer 15 to 20 minutes before serving. Makes 12 servings.

When you put away groceries, be sure to label any ingredients that are intended for dinner...that way, Wednesday's supper won't turn into Tuesday's after-school snack! Set aside cubed cheese, veggies and fruit labeled "OK for snacking" to tame appetites.

Healthy Bites For Snacking

Raspberry-Peach Yogurt Pops

Cindy Jamieson
Barrie, Ontario

These pops came from my effort to create a healthy cold treat for my kids. Now they enjoy helping me make these pops with raspberries picked in our backyard garden.

2 6-oz. containers low-fat
    peach yogurt
2 T. milk
2 T. honey

1/4 c. fresh raspberries
4 5-oz. freezer treat molds or
    paper cups with treat sticks

In a bowl, combine yogurt, milk and honey; stir well to combine. Crush raspberries with a fork, leaving some pieces whole. Stir crushed berries into yogurt mixture. Pour into molds or cups; insert sticks. Cover and freeze until completely frozen. To remove, dip into warm water for a few seconds. Makes 4 servings.

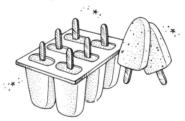

Banana-Orange Yogurt Pops

Sheila Plock
Boalsburg, PA

A healthy after-school treat to enjoy on a hot day.

16-oz. container vanilla or
    plain yogurt
6-oz. can frozen orange juice
    concentrate, thawed

2 ripe bananas, sliced
Optional: sweetener to taste
8 5-oz. freezer treat molds or
    paper cups with treat sticks

In a blender, combine yogurt, orange juice concentrate and bananas. Process on medium speed until smooth. Pour into molds or paper cups. Freeze one hour and then insert sticks. Cover and freeze until completely frozen. To remove, dip into warm water for a few seconds. Makes 8 servings.

Chili-Cheese Dip

Jeanne Hunt
Oswego, NY

Always a hit no matter what the occasion! My kids request this often and it's so quick & easy, I'm happy to make it. I started adding the diced jalapeños as they got older. When my daughter Lauren was 12 and needed a snack to take camping, this was simple enough for her to make. Now that she's grown and living on her own, she makes it for her friends and they request it often.

8-oz. pkg. cream cheese,
   softened
15-oz. can turkey chili, with or
   without beans
2 c. finely shredded Cheddar
   cheese

Optional: 1 to 2 jalapeño
   peppers, seeded and minced
scoop-type corn chips

Spread cream cheese evenly in the bottom of a microwave-safe 9" glass pie plate. Spread chili over cream cheese; sprinkle cheese evenly over chili. Sprinkle jalapeños over cheese, if desired. Microwave on high for 5 to 6 minutes, until bubbly and cheese melts. May also be baked at 350 degrees for 20 to 25 minutes. Serve warm with corn chips. Serves 6 to 8.

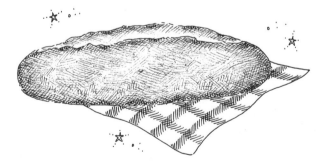

Bruschetta is an easy, delicious snack...and kids will giggle learning to say broo-SKETT-a! Dice two sun-ripe tomatoes and mix with a teaspoon of olive oil and 1/2 teaspoon chopped fresh basil. Spread over toasted slices of Italian bread.

Healthy Bites
For Snacking

Easy Cheesy Quesadillas

Kathie High
Lititz, PA

Your kids will love you for making these tasty quesadillas...you will love how simple it is! These are great to dip in hot soup.

8 8-inch flour tortillas, divided

8-oz. pkg. shredded Cheddar cheese

Place 4 tortillas on an ungreased baking sheet; top with shredded cheese. Top each tortilla with a second tortilla. Bake, uncovered, at 450 degrees for about 4 to 5 minutes, until toasty and cheese is melted. Cut each into 4 quarters. Serves 4.

Not Yo' Nachos

Donna Tennant
Jasper, IN

This is the first recipe I showed my 6-year-old niece Kathy how to make. She loves it and it has spread family-wide. She told me, "Aunt Dee-Dee, these taste like they came from a fancy place!"

40 scoop-type tortilla chips
9-oz. can bean dip
8-oz. pkg. shredded Cheddar
   cheese

Optional: sour cream, diced jalapeño peppers

Spread chips on an ungreased baking sheet. Fill each chip with bean dip; top with cheese. Bake, uncovered, at 425 degrees for 10 minutes, or until cheese melts. Serve hot, topped with sour cream and jalapeños, if desired. Serves 4.

Paper coffee filters make tidy holders for tacos and tortilla wraps...easy for little hands to hold too.

Mini Bean Dip Jars

Sonya Labbe
West Hollywood, CA

I came up with this recipe for my uncle, who prefers not to share a communal dip bowl. Now, everybody can enjoy their own yummy cup of dip. Use plastic containers if you prefer...terrific for tucking into lunchboxes!

2 tomatoes, finely chopped
1/2 c. onion, finely chopped
1/2 t. coarse salt
2 ripe avocados, halved, pitted
　　and peeled
1 to 2 pickled jalapeño peppers,
　　minced
1 T. lime juice

1 c. plus 2 T. sour cream,
　　divided
2　16-oz. cans refried beans
1 c. shredded Cheddar cheese
6-oz. can chopped black olives,
　　drained
8　8-oz. canning jars with lids
tortilla chips

In a bowl, mix tomatoes with onion and salt; set aside. In a separate bowl, mash avocados with jalapeños, lime juice and 2 tablespoons sour cream. In the bottom of each jar, spread a half-inch layer of refried beans. Layer each jar with 2 tablespoons cheese, one tablespoon tomato mixture, 3 tablespoons avocado mixture, 2 tablespoons sour cream and 2 tablespoons olives. Add lids, if not serving immediately. Serve with tortilla chips. Makes 8 servings.

A crockery bowl filled to the brim with ripe pears, apples and other fresh fruit makes an oh-so-simple centerpiece... it's a great way to encourage healthy snacking too!

Healthy Bites
For Snacking

Cheesy Fiesta Bites

Amy Hunt
Traphill, NC

These tasty puffs are quick snacks for after-school and on-the-go...great party appetizers too.

4 eggs, beaten
1/2 c. thick and chunky salsa
1/4 c. all-purpose flour
2 t. chili powder
1 green onion, chopped

1-1/2 c. shredded Cheddar
   cheese
Garnish: sour cream, additional
   salsa

Spray 24 mini muffin cups with non-stick vegetable spray; set aside. In a large bowl, mix eggs, salsa, flour and chili powder until well blended. Stir in onion and cheese. Spoon mixture into muffin cups by tablespoonfuls. Bake at 400 degrees for 10 minutes, or until golden. Garnish as desired. Makes 2 dozen.

A three-year-old child is a being who gets almost as much fun out of a 56-dollar set of swings as it does out of finding a small green worm.

–Bill Vaughan

Snackin' Pizza Sticks

Tracy Stoll
Seville, OH

Super quick & easy...the kids can help put them together!

11-oz. can refrigerated
   bread sticks
24 pepperoni slices
2 T. grated Parmesan cheese

1/2 t. Italian seasoning
1/4 t. garlic powder
1/2 c. pizza sauce, warmed

Unroll bread sticks and separate. Over half of each bread stick, place 3 pepperoni slices. Fold remaining half of bread stick over top; seal end and twist. Place on an ungreased baking sheet. Combine cheese and seasonings in a cup; sprinkle evenly over each bread stick. Bake at 350 degrees for 15 to 20 minutes, until golden. Serve with warm pizza sauce. Makes 8 servings.

Freaky-face pizza snacks! Let the kids make faces with
toppings such as pepperoni and tomato "eyes,"
carrot curl "hair" and green pepper "smiles."

Healthy Bites
For Snacking

Italian Cheese Fries

Anne Alesauskas
Minocqua, WI

When I was growing up, we had a local pizza place that served the best Italian fries ever! In fact, I'm not sure that I've ever had their pizza, only their Italian fries. This is a fairly close duplicate for those times when I'm craving that blast from the past.

13.8-oz. tube refrigerated
   pizza dough
2 to 3 t. olive oil
2 c. shredded mozzarella cheese

1 t. garlic powder
1 t. Italian seasoning
Garnish: marinara sauce,
   ranch salad dressing

Line a baking sheet with aluminum foil and spray with non-stick vegetable spray. Roll out pizza dough on baking sheet; brush with olive oil. Top with cheese and seasonings. Bake at 425 degrees for 10 to 12 minutes, until crust is golden and cheese is bubbly. Cut into strips; serve warm with marinara sauce or salad dressing, or both. Serves 4.

Are your refrigerator doors overwhelmed with youthful crayon masterpieces? Select a few special drawings to have matted and framed...the kids will be so proud!

Quick & Easy Mini Pizzas

Amanda Johnson
Marysville, OH

My two boys Evan and Ben love these little pizzas for a really fast after-school snack. My husband Rob loves these pizzas too!

4 slices bread, crusts trimmed
1/2 c. pizza sauce
1/2 c. shredded mozzarella
   cheese, divided

16 pepperoni slices
Optional: other pizza toppings

Roll each slice of bread flat with a rolling pin. Cut into circles with a large biscuit cutter, if desired. Divide sauce, cheese and pepperoni among bread slices. Add other toppings, if desired. Place on a baking sheet sprayed with non-stick vegetable spray. Bake at 375 degrees for 10 to 12 minutes, until crisp and golden. Makes 4 servings.

Grow a pizza garden! Create a round garden sectioned into wedges. Plant basil, oregano and parsley...add some tomatoes, peppers and onions. A terrific way to get kids interested in fresh foods!

Healthy Bites
For Snacking

MacKenley's Cheesy Dip

Linda Stone
Cookeville, TN

My grandson loves this simple dip...his other grandmother
and I both make it for him often. Adults like it too!

8-oz. pkg. cream cheese,
  softened
8-oz. can mild or hot picante
  sauce

1 to 1-1/2 c. shredded Cheddar
  cheese
tortilla chips

Place cream cheese in a 13"x9" glass baking pan or other microwave-safe dish that fits your microwave. Cook on high setting for one to 1-1/2 minutes, until cream cheese is softened; spread evenly over bottom of pan. Pour picante sauce over cream cheese; microwave for 2 minutes, or until hot. Top with shredded cheese. Serve with tortilla chips. Makes 8 servings.

Create a comfy spot where kids can read their favorite books after school, or just daydream...a window seat topped with a cushion. Add some soft pillows and a cozy throw.

Delicious Dip for Fruit

JoAnn

*Kids can have fun making rainbow fruit skewers to eat
with this sweet and simple dip.*

1 c. plain Greek yogurt
2 T. brown sugar, packed
1 t. vanilla extract

fruit slices or chunks,
whole strawberries

Combine yogurt, brown sugar and vanilla in a bowl. Stir until brown
sugar is dissolved; cover and keep refrigerated. Serve with fruit. Makes
3 to 4 servings.

Make banana pops for a frosty treat! Spread a banana with
fruit-flavored yogurt, sprinkle with nuts and place on a tray
to freeze. Once frozen, wrap in plastic wrap and return to
freezer for a cool snack anytime.

Healthy Bites
For Snacking

Crispy Apple Chips

Gladys Kielar
Whitehouse, OH

Here is a sweet and healthy snack to make at home...you'll love it!

4 apples, sliced crosswise, 1/8-inch thick

Remove seeds from apple slices. Arrange slices on 2 parchment paper-lined baking sheets. Bake at 225 degrees for one to 1-1/2 hours. Turn slices over; continue baking about one hour longer, until crisp. Remove to a wire rack; cool completely. Store chips in an airtight container up to one week. Makes 2 to 3 servings.

Paper Bag Popcorn

Kathy Grashoff
Fort Wayne, IN

Very quick to fix...budget-friendly and healthy too! We like to add Cajun seasoning, but feel free to add your own favorite.

1/4 c. popcorn kernels
1/2 t. peanut or canola oil
1/4 t. salt

1 brown paper lunch bag
Optional: spray butter,
additional salt

Toss together popcorn, oil and salt in a bowl. Transfer to bag; fold over 3 to 4 times to close. Set bag on a microwave-safe plate. Microwave on high until kernels stop popping, about 2 minutes. Season with spray butter and more salt, if desired. Makes one to 2 servings.

Find a reason to celebrate! Kids will love it when you recognize their achievements... an A in math, the game-winning goal or a new Scout badge... in a big way.

Vegetable Medley with Sour Cream Dip

Carolin Oberle-Balz
Weinheim, Germany

My mom used to make this dip for family gatherings when we were kids. When I found the recipe in her old handwritten cookbook, I simply had to try it out. It still tastes just as good and our children, our friends and their children all love it. Thanks, Mom!

1/2 c. sour cream
8-oz. pkg. cream cheese, softened
1 t. mustard
1 t. salt, or to taste
1 t. pepper, or to taste
1 green pepper, finely chopped

1 tomato, finely chopped
1 bunch green onions, thinly sliced
cauliflower, cucumber, carrots, celery and cherry tomatoes, cut into bite-size slices or cubes

In a bowl, mix together sour cream and cream cheese until smooth; add mustard, salt and pepper. Stir in green pepper, tomato and green onions. Cover and chill for several hours to overnight. Serve with a variety of cut-up vegetables for dipping. Serves 4 to 8.

"Sandwich sushi" is sure to be a hit for after-school snacking or in lunchboxes. Spread tortillas with cream cheese and layer on sliced deli meat and spinach leaves, or other favorite foods...there are lots of possibilities. Roll up tightly and slice into easy-to-handle pieces.

Healthy Bites
For Snacking

Yummy Hummus

Eleanor Dionne
Beverly, MA

Snackers of all ages will enjoy this dip! I love to make it because it's delicious and nutritious, especially when I am watching my carb intake. Red pepper strips are my favorite for dipping.

1 to 2 cloves garlic
2 19-oz. cans garbanzo beans,
    drained
2 T. tahini paste
2 T. lemon juice
1/4 c. olive oil

1/4 c. water
1/4 t. ground cumin
salt and pepper
red pepper strips or other cut-up
    vegetables

Add garlic to a food processor; process until finely chopped. Add beans and remaining ingredients except vegetables; process until smooth. Use a spatula to remove hummus to a serving bowl. Serve immediately with cut-up vegetables, or cover and chill. Makes about 2 cups.

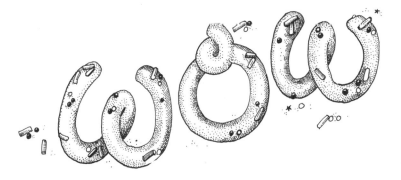

Can you spell YUM? Refrigerated bread sticks present all kinds of alphabet fun...just shape the dough into letters before baking! Sprinkle with cinnamon-sugar for a sweet treat.

School Fuel Snack Mix

Beth Bundy
Long Prairie, MN

*My kids love to help in the kitchen! This is one sweet treat
they gladly make over & over again. Pack it up in mini
paper lunchbags for snacks-to-go.*

3/4 c. brown sugar, packed
6 T. butter, sliced
3 T. light corn syrup
1/4 t. baking soda
4 c. bite-size crispy corn cereal
squares

4 c. bite-size crispy rice cereal
squares
1/2 c. semi-sweet chocolate
chips

Cover a baking sheet with wax paper; set aside. In a large microwave-safe bowl, heat brown sugar, butter and corn syrup on high for one to 2 minutes, until butter is melted. Stir well. Stir in baking soda until dissolved. Stir in cereals until coated. Microwave on high for 3 minutes, stirring after every minute. Spread out onto prepared baking sheet. Let cool for 10 minutes; break into bite-size pieces. In a small microwave-safe bowl, microwave chocolate chips on high for one to 1-1/2 minutes; stir until smooth and drizzle over snack mix. Refrigerate until chocolate is set. Store in an air-tight container. Makes 8 cups.

Make tonight a family game night! Get out all your favorite
board games and play to your heart's content.

Healthy Bites
For Snacking

Mrs. Nelson's Caramel Corn

Chris McCain
Mosinee, WI

My high school librarian was a great mentor to me. She shared this recipe with me over 25 years ago. It is easy and kid-friendly. My grandkids love to sing "Shake, shake, shake" as we shake the bag. Every time I make this I'm thankful that I had a great lady like Mrs. Nelson in my life for friendship and guidance.

3 to 4 qts. popped corn
1 brown paper grocery bag
1 c. brown sugar, packed
1/2 c. butter

1/4 c. light corn syrup
1/2 t. salt
1/2 t. baking soda

Place popcorn in a brown paper grocery bag; discard any unpopped kernels and set aside. In a 2-quart microwave-safe dish, combine brown sugar, butter, corn syrup and salt. Microwave on high at 2-minute intervals until boiling; continue microwaving for 2 minutes. Remove from microwave; stir in baking soda. Pour mixture over corn; fold over top of bag and shake well. Microwave bag on high for 1-1/2 minutes. Shake again; microwave another 1-1/2 to 2-1/2 minutes. Pour popcorn into a serving bowl; let cool. Store in an airtight container. Makes 3 to 4 quarts.

Parade Snack Mix

Beth Bundy
Long Prairie, MN

My kids love this snack mix! It's our tradition to make a double batch, scoop it into little bags and head to a parade... to share with friends, of course!

1 c. mini bear-shaped graham
   crackers
1 c. animal crackers
1 c. mini pretzel twists

1 c. candy-coated chocolates
1 c. yogurt-covered raisins
1 c. salted peanuts

In a large bowl, combine all ingredients; mix well. Store in an airtight container. Makes 6 cups.

Mom's Frosty Fruit Drink

Janet Hanley
Manassas, VA

After their swim meets, my children always wanted to stop at the convenience store for a slushy drink. Trying to cut the cost of buying four drinks several times a week, I decided to make my own. It has been a family favorite for years...tastes just the same! Try lemonade, punch, grape or any other juice in the freezer section.

12-oz. can frozen fruit juice   ice cubes
    concentrate

Spoon frozen juice concentrate into a blender. Add enough ice to fill up the blender; process until slushy. Serve immediately. Serves 4.

Grandma's Orangeade

Cris Goode
Mooresville, IN

This is Grandma's way of making a fruity soft drink mix more delicious and nutritious!

12-oz. can frozen orange juice   1/4 c. sugar
    concentrate, thawed   0.15-oz. env. unsweetened
1 gal. water   orange drink mix

Mix all ingredients in a large pitcher; chill. Stir each time before serving. Makes about one gallon.

Save bananas that are getting too ripe. Peel, cut into chunks, wrap in plastic wrap and tuck in the freezer. Later they can be tossed into smoothies... no thawing needed.

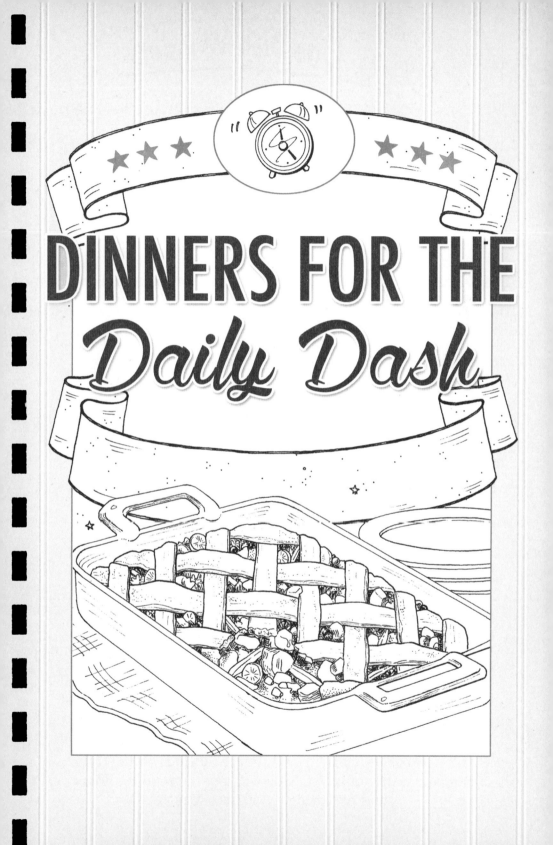

DINNERS FOR THE
Daily Dash

Cheesy Enchilada Chicken & Rice

Ann Mathis
Biscoe, AR

This is an easy casserole that my children love...most adults do too!
It's perfect to take to anyone who's under the weather or
just in need of some comfort food.

18-1/2 oz. can chicken-cheese
   enchilada soup
1-3/4 c. water
3/4 c. long-cooking white or
   brown rice, uncooked
15-oz. can pinto beans, drained
   and rinsed

11-oz. can sweet corn & diced
   peppers, drained
1/2 t. ground cumin
1/4 t. pepper
1 to 1-1/2 lbs. boneless, skinless
   chicken breasts
1 c. shredded Colby-Jack cheese

In an ungreased 2-quart glass casserole dish, mix soup, water, uncooked rice, beans, corn and seasonings. Arrange chicken on top. Cover and bake at 375 degrees for about 30 minutes, until rice is tender and chicken juices run clear when pierced. Stir rice mixture around chicken; sprinkle with cheese. Bake, uncovered, an additional 5 to 10 minutes, until cheese is melted. Serves 6.

Create a meal plan for one or even two weeks, including all of your family's favorite quick & easy meals...spaghetti on Monday, tacos on Tuesday and so forth. Post it on the fridge along with a shopping list. Kids will look forward to dinner, and preparing it will be a snap.

Dinners for the
Daily Dash

Southwest Chicken Skillet

Pat Wissler
Harrisburg, PA

This is so good and easy...a perfect kid-friendly weeknight meal!

2 T. oil
1-1/4 lbs. boneless, skinless
  chicken breasts, cubed
16-oz. pkg. frozen broccoli,
  red pepper, onion and
  mushroom stir-fry mix

15-oz. can black beans, drained
  and rinsed
1 c. chunky salsa
8-inch flour tortilla, cut into
  2-inch by 1-inch strips
1 c. shredded Cheddar cheese

In a skillet, heat oil over medium-high heat. Cook chicken for 3 to
4 minutes, stirring occasionally, until no longer pink in the center. Stir
in frozen vegetables, beans and salsa; reduce heat to medium. Cover
and cook for 6 to 8 minutes, stirring occasionally, until vegetables are
crisp-tender. Sprinkle with tortilla strips and cheese. Cover and cook
about 2 minutes, or until cheese is melted. Serves 4.

Cheesy Chicken Enchiladas

Sarah Bruner
Roundup, MT

Even the kids love this hearty recipe! It's mild tasting, they get to
help cook dinner and there are no "ickies" like onions or peppers.

2 8-oz. cans mild red or green
  enchilada sauce, divided
2 to 2-1/2 c. cooked rice
10 10-inch flour tortillas

2 boneless, skinless chicken
  breasts, grilled and shredded
16-oz. pkg. shredded Mexican-
  blend cheese, divided

Spread half of one can sauce in a lightly greased 13"x9" baking pan;
set aside. Mix remaining half can of sauce with cooked rice. Fill each
tortilla with one heaping spoonful rice mixture, one heaping spoonful
chicken and a generous sprinkle of cheese. Fold in 2 sides of tortilla,
then the top; roll tightly. Arrange enchiladas over sauce in baking pan.
Top with remaining can of sauce and remaining cheese. Bake,
uncovered, at 400 degrees for 20 minutes, or until cheese is melted;
let stand for 5 to 10 minutes. Serves 5.

Italian Chicken & Penne Skillet

Vickie

A skilletful of flavorful goodness in less than 30 minutes! For variety, sometimes I'll add sliced mushrooms or canned artichokes, or use rotini twirls instead of penne pasta.

16-oz. pkg. penne pasta, uncooked and divided
1 to 2 T. olive oil
3/4 lb. boneless, skinless chicken breast, cut into 1-inch strips
1 to 2 zucchini, quartered and thinly sliced
1/2 c. onion, chopped
2 cloves garlic, minced
14-1/2 oz. can diced tomatoes with Italian herbs, drained
1/2 t. salt
Garnish: grated Parmesan cheese

Cook half of the pasta according to package directions; drain. Reserve uncooked pasta for use in another recipe. Meanwhile, heat oil in a large skillet over medium heat; cook chicken until lightly golden. Add zucchini, onion and garlic; cook and stir until tender-crisp, 3 to 4 minutes. Add tomatoes and salt; cook and stir until heated through. Gently stir in cooked pasta. Serve topped with Parmesan cheese. Serves 4.

Perfect pasta every time! Fill a large pot with water and bring to a rolling boil. Add one tablespoon of salt, if desired. Stir in pasta; return to a rolling boil. Boil, uncovered, for the time recommended on the package. There's no need to add oil... frequent stirring will keep pasta from sticking together.

Dinners for the
Daily Dash

Baked Chicken Cacciatore

Julie Gasparro
Scottsdale, AZ

My family's favorite dinner! I make it at least twice a month and no wonder...it's delicious and you don't even have to precook the pasta! Use your own homemade sauce or a favorite store brand.

6 boneless, skinless chicken
   breasts
3 green and/or red peppers,
   chopped
2 onions, chopped
4 cloves garlic, chopped
16-oz. pkg. penne pasta,
   uncooked

4 c. spaghetti sauce
1 c. water
8-oz. pkg. shredded mozzarella
   cheese
1/4 c. shredded Parmesan
   cheese

Arrange chicken in a well-greased 13"x9" baking pan. Arrange peppers and onions around chicken. Add uncooked pasta, pushing down around chicken and vegetables. Pour sauce evenly over all; drizzle with water. Cover completely with heavy-duty aluminum foil, sealing edges tightly around pan so no steam can escape. Bake at 350 degrees for one hour. Uncover and sprinkle with cheeses. Bake, uncovered, for another 20 to 30 minutes. Serve pasta mixture topped with chicken. Makes 6 servings.

Create a cozy Italian restaurant feel for dinner. Toss a red & white checked tablecloth over the table, light drip candles in empty bottles and add a basket of garlic bread. Great for getting kids to practice their table manners!

One-Pan Spaghetti

Deb Kidd
Gladwin, MI

This recipe is great for any busy family. After you've worked all day, then picked the kids up from school, dinner can simmer while you help them with homework or just sit and relax a bit.

1 lb. ground beef, broken up
2 c. spaghetti, uncooked and
　broken into 1-inch pieces
1/2 to 1 c. onion, chopped

1 clove garlic, minced
28-oz. can crushed tomatoes
Optional: 1 T. sugar

In a large deep skillet, layer uncooked beef, spaghetti, onion, garlic, tomatoes with juice and sugar, if using. Cover and cook over high heat until steam appears around the edges. Stir; reduce heat to medium-low. Cover and simmer for about 30 minutes, stirring occasionally, until beef is cooked and spaghetti is tender. Serves 4.

Cheeseburger Meatballs

Sheila Gwaltney
Johnson City, TN

My kids eat these meatballs without one complaint...adults like them too! Once I even made 200 servings for a wedding I catered and everyone raved about them.

1/2 c. pasteurized process
　cheese sauce
1/4 c. catsup
1/2 c. milk or water

12-1/2 oz. pkg. frozen beef or
　turkey meatballs
Optional: 1/2 c. onion, chopped
cooked rice or pasta

Mix cheese sauce, catsup and milk or water in a skillet. Bring to a boil over medium heat. Stir in meatballs and onion, if using. Reduce heat to medium-low. Simmer for 15 minutes, stirring occasionally, until sauce is thickened. Serve over rice or pasta. Serves 4.

Dinners for the
Daily Dash

Sandy's Pizza Casserole

Barbara Imler
Noblesville, IN

This is a very kid-friendly casserole and tasty for adults, too!
That makes it ideal to take to a carry-in dinner.

16-oz. pkg. elbow macaroni,
  uncooked
1 lb. ground beef
Optional: 1 c. mixed chopped
  onion, mushrooms and
  green pepper

1/2 t. garlic powder
4-oz. pkg. sliced pepperoni,
  slices halved
24-oz. jar spaghetti sauce
16-oz. jar Cheddar cheese
  pasta sauce

Cook macaroni according to package directions. Drain; place in a greased 13"x9" baking pan. Meanwhile, in a skillet over medium heat, brown beef with vegetables, if using. Drain; sprinkle with garlic powder. Top cooked macaroni with beef mixture, pepperoni and tomato pasta sauce. Add cheese pasta sauce and stir gently. Bake, uncovered, at 350 degrees for 35 to 45 minutes, until hot and bubbly. Makes 8 servings.

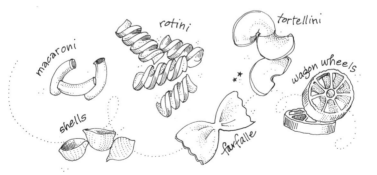

When a recipe calls for pasta, there are lots of shapes to choose from. Let the kids take turns picking out different kinds, and give a favorite dish a whole new look!

Black Bean & Corn Enchilada Stack

Marie Matter
Dallas, TX

This is a simple, hearty vegetarian dish that our family loves.
It's cheesy, it's spicy, it's just so good!

2 15-oz. cans black beans,
   drained and rinsed
15-oz. can red enchilada sauce,
   divided
1 c. frozen corn, thawed
4 jalapeño peppers, seeded
   and diced
1/2 t. chili powder

1/2 t. garlic powder
1/2 t. kosher salt
1/8 t. cayenne pepper
1 c. shredded Pepper Jack
   cheese, divided
12 6-inch corn tortillas
Optional: sliced green onions

In a large bowl, combine beans, one cup enchilada sauce, corn, jalapeños, seasonings and 1/2 cup cheese; set aside. Spray an 8"x8" baking pan with non-stick vegetable spray. Add a small amount of remaining sauce to the bottom of pan, swirling to coat. Layer 4 tortillas over sauce; add half of bean mixture. Repeat layering with a little more sauce, 4 tortillas and remaining bean mixture. Add remaining tortillas, sauce and cheese. Bake, uncovered, at 400 degrees for 20 to 25 minutes, until hot and bubbly. Remove pan to a wire rack; let stand for about 5 minutes. Garnish with green onions, if desired. Serves 4.

Dried beans come in lots of varieties, and they're easy to prepare in a slow cooker. Cover beans with water and add a teaspoon of baking soda. Cover and cook on low setting for 8 hours to overnight. Drain well and use immediately, or cover and refrigerate for up to 3 days.

Dinners for the
Daily Dash

Cowgirl Hot Pot

Becky Drees
Pittsfield, MA

The flavor of the Gouda cheese really shines in this recipe.
A delicious comfort-food meal and it's meatless!

1 onion, chopped
1 red pepper, chopped
2 carrots, peeled and chopped
3 T. oil
14-oz. can smoky baked beans
1 c. green beans, chopped
8-1/2 oz. can corn
1/3 c. tomato paste
1/2 c. barbecue sauce
1 t. seasoned salt
1/4 lb. smoked Gouda cheese, cubed
1-1/2 c. frozen shredded hashbrowns
1/4 c. butter, melted
salt and pepper

In a large deep skillet over medium heat, sauté onion, red pepper and carrots in oil until softened but not browned. Add beans, corn with liquid, tomato paste, barbecue sauce and salt. Bring to a boil; reduce heat to medium-low and simmer for 5 minutes. Transfer vegetable mixture to a lightly greased, shallow 2-1/2 quart casserole dish; scatter cheese over top. In a bowl, mix hashbrowns and melted butter. Spread hashbrown mixture over vegetable mixture. Season with salt and pepper. Bake, uncovered, at 375 degrees for 40 to 45 minutes, until hashbrowns are tender and golden. Makes 6 to 8 servings.

Create mini recipe cards listing the ingredients of favorite one-dish dinners. Glue a button magnet on the back and place on the fridge...so handy whenever it's time to make out a shopping list!

Turkey-Broccoli Casserole

Janelle DeWitt
Grant, IA

When I was a kid, every Wednesday night we knew we'd be having this hearty dish for supper. Even now, it still makes my mouth water!

16-oz. pkg. frozen broccoli
2 lbs. ground turkey
8-oz. pkg. sliced mushrooms
1 onion, chopped
salt and pepper to taste

2 10-3/4 oz. cans cream of
    celery soup
16-oz. container sour cream
16-oz. pkg. shredded Monterey
    Jack cheese

Prepare broccoli according to package directions; drain well. Meanwhile, in a large deep skillet over medium heat, brown turkey with mushrooms and onion; drain. Season turkey mixture with salt and pepper; stir in soup and sour cream. Reduce heat to low; heat through. Transfer mixture to a lightly greased 13"x9" baking pan. Layer evenly with broccoli; top with cheese. Bake, uncovered, at 350 degrees for one hour, until bubbly and lightly golden. Makes 8 to 10 servings.

Often, there's quite a lot going on in the kitchen as you're preparing the family's dinner. Be sure to set a kitchen timer as you slip the casserole in the oven...let it watch the clock so you don't have to.

Dinners for the
Daily Dash

Wendy's Sticky Chicky

Wendy Reaume
Chatham, Ontario

If you're looking to replace your favorite Chinese take-out with a healthier and cheaper option, this recipe is perfect for you.

1 to 2 T. olive oil
7 to 8 boneless, skinless chicken
   thighs, cubed
salt and pepper to taste
3/4 c. soy sauce
1/3 c. rice vinegar
1/3 c. honey
3 T. brown sugar, packed

1 T. fresh ginger, peeled
   and grated
1 t. sesame oil
4 cloves garlic, minced
hot pepper sauce to taste
cooked white or brown rice
Garnish: chopped green onions

Heat olive oil in a large skillet over medium heat. Cook chicken until golden and juices run clear. In a bowl, stir together remaining ingredients except rice and garnish. Add mixture to skillet. Cook over medium-low heat until sauce starts to thicken, about 8 to 10 minutes, stirring often. Serve chicken and sauce over cooked rice; garnish with green onions. Makes 6 servings.

Real cloth napkins make mealtime just a little more special, and they're earth-friendly too...no paper napkins to throw away. Stitch fun charms to napkin rings, so everyone can identify their own napkin easily.

Mother's Taco Casserole

Emily Cole
Grafton, OH

My mom shared this recipe with me...my kids and husband love it!
It's easy for a quick evening meal or even a party.

1 lb. ground beef
1-1/4 oz. pkg. taco seasoning
   mix
2/3 c. water
1 to 2 16-oz. cans refried beans

8-oz. pkg. cream cheese, cubed
16-oz. jar mild picante sauce
2 c. shredded Cheddar cheese
tortilla chips

Brown beef in a skillet over medium heat; drain. Stir in taco seasoning and water; bring to a boil. Reduce heat to low; simmer for 5 to 7 minutes. Meanwhile, spread beans in a greased 13"x9" baking pan. Layer with cream cheese, beef mixture, picante sauce and Cheddar cheese. Bake, uncovered, at 350 degrees for 25 minutes, or until bubbly and cheese is melted. Serve with tortilla chips. Makes 6 to 8 servings.

Quick Chili Bake

Carolyn Deckard
Bedford, IN

My daughter Sherry Lynn gave me this fast recipe. She fixes it
often with all the kids after their school projects.

7-oz. pkg. rotini pasta,
   uncooked
15-oz. can chili
12-oz. jar mild or medium
   chunky salsa

12-oz. can corn, drained
1/2 c. shredded Cheddar cheese
Optional: corn chips

Cook pasta according to package directions, just until tender; drain. In a large bowl, combine chili, salsa and corn. Add cooked pasta; toss to coat. Spoon into a lightly greased 2-quart casserole; top with cheese. Bake, uncovered, at 400 degrees for about 30 minutes, until hot and bubbly. Serve with corn chips, if desired. Makes 6 servings.

Dinners for the
Daily Dash

Happy Burritos

Ruth Hebert
Houma, LA

*I've been serving these burritos since my six children
were school-age...always a favorite!*

2 to 3 lbs. lean ground beef
16-oz. can refried beans
1-1/4 oz. pkg. taco
   seasoning mix
10 10-inch flour tortillas

2 15-oz. cans chili without
   beans
16-oz. pkg. shredded Cheddar
   cheese

Brown beef in a skillet over medium heat; drain. Stir in refried beans
and taco seasoning. Spoon beef mixture into tortillas; roll up and place
seam-side down in a greased 13"x9" baking pan. Spoon chili over top;
sprinkle with cheese. Bake, uncovered, at 350 degrees for one hour.
Serves 6 generously.

Southwestern Goulash

Tina George
El Dorado, AR

*Being a busy mom & gramma, I turn often to my own
quick & easy recipes. This dish is simple and oh-so good!
Serve with cornbread or cheesy tortillas.*

2 c. elbow macaroni, uncooked
1 lb. ground beef
1 t. ground cumin
1 t. chili powder
1 c. frozen corn, thawed

14-1/2 oz. can diced tomatoes
10-oz. can diced tomatoes with
   green chiles
1 c. shredded Mexican-blend
   cheese

Cook macaroni according to package directions; drain. Meanwhile,
brown beef in a skillet over medium heat; drain. Stir in seasonings,
corn and tomatoes with liquid. Simmer for several minutes, until
heated through. Stir in cooked macaroni. Reduce heat to medium-low;
cover and simmer for 10 to 15 minutes. Top with cheese. Serves 6.

Sweet Potato-Corn Dog Bake

Tearie Swoboda
Clarksville, TN

This dish was created by trial & error with my grandson Eric. It's kid-friendly and fun as well as sneaking a little healthy in there.

3 c. sweet potatoes, peeled,
  cooked and mashed
1 lb. hot dogs or smoked
  sausage, diced
1 onion, diced
1/2 green or red pepper, diced
2 to 3 t. oil

2 8-1/2 oz. pkgs. corn muffin
  mix
2 eggs, beaten
2/3 c. milk
1/2 c. frozen corn
14-3/4 oz. can creamed corn

Spread sweet potatoes in the bottom of a lightly greased 13"x9" baking pan; set aside. In a skillet, sauté hot dogs or sausage, onion and pepper in oil until onion is tender, about 5 minutes. Spread hot dog mixture over sweet potatoes. In a bowl, combine dry corn muffin mix, eggs, milk and corn; mix well and spread over top. Bake, uncovered, at 400 degrees for 30 minutes, or until topping tests clean with a knife tip. Let stand for 5 minutes before cutting. Makes 6 servings.

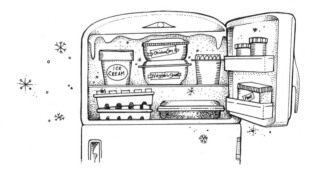

Get a head start on dinner. Assemble a casserole the night before, cover and refrigerate. Just add 15 to 20 minutes to the baking time...the casserole is ready to serve when it's hot and bubbly in the center.

Dinners for the Daily Dash

Cheesy Ham & Potato Bake

Sharon Beaty
Boonville, IN

This dish is a favorite standby for my hungry family. With eight children, a fast crowd-pleasing meal is always welcome!

8 potatoes
1 c. cooked ham, shredded
1/2 c. dried, chopped onion
10-3/4 oz. can of mushroom
   soup

1/2 c. milk
1/3 c. olive oil
1-1/2 t. salt
1 T. pepper
1 c. shredded Cheddar cheese

In a large saucepan, cover unpeeled potatoes with water. Cook over medium-high heat until tender, about 15 to 20 minutes. Cool; pull off peels. Shred potatoes; spread in a 13"x9" baking pan sprayed with non-stick vegetable spray. In a bowl, combine remaining ingredients except cheese; stir gently and spread over potatoes. Top with cheese. Bake, uncovered, at 350 degrees for about 30 minutes, until bubbly and cheese is melted. Makes 8 servings.

Pour vegetable oil into a plastic squeeze bottle.
This makes it easy to drizzle oil just where it's needed,
with no waste and no mess.

Cheesy Tuna Skillet

Kristin Pittis
Dennison, OH

*This is my go-to meal when I want something quick & easy
that doesn't use many pots & pans. Even my picky husband
and my toddler like it!*

14-oz. can chicken broth
1-3/4 c. water
16-oz. pkg. rotini pasta,
　uncooked
10-3/4 oz. can of mushroom
　soup
1 c. milk

2.6-oz. pkg. chunk light tuna,
　flaked
1 c. shredded Cheddar cheese
1 c. shredded mozzarella cheese
1/2 c. seasoned dry bread
　crumbs
2 T. butter, melted

In a large non-stick skillet, bring broth and water to a boil; stir in
pasta. Return to a boil and cook for 6 to 7 minutes; do not drain. Stir
in soup, milk and tuna. Reduce heat to medium-low. Cover and cook,
stirring frequently, until pasta is tender, adding a little more milk
if needed. Stir in cheeses; cook until melted. In a small bowl, mix
together bread crumbs and butter; sprinkle over pasta mixture.
Serves 6.

While dinner is cooking, mix up some good clean fun with
homemade bubble solution! Stir together 5 cups water, 2 cups
dishwashing liquid and 1/2 cup light corn syrup. Let the kids
explore the kitchen for pancake turners, strainers and other
utensils to use as bubble wands.

Dinners for the *Daily Dash*

Salmon Pea Wiggle

Shirley Howie
Foxboro, MA

An old New England favorite whose name is sure to make kids giggle! Try it with tuna instead of salmon...serve over rice or toast for added variety. All combinations are quick, easy and delicious!

1/4 c. butter, sliced	15-oz. can peas, drained
1/4 c. all-purpose flour	6-oz. can salmon, drained
1/2 t. salt	and flaked
1/4 t. pepper	2 c. wide egg noodles, cooked
2 c. milk	and drained

Melt butter over low heat in a heavy saucepan. Blend in flour, salt, and pepper. Cook and stir until mixture is smooth and bubbly. Stir in milk. Bring to a boil, stirring constantly; boil for one minute. Stir in peas and salmon; heat through. Serve over cooked noodles. Makes 4 servings.

A real kitchen time-saver! A silicon hot pad can function as trivet, potholder, anti-slip pad for mixing bowls, jar opener and garlic peeler.

Citrus Baked Fish

Debra Arch
Kewanee, IL

My kids will eat fish when it's prepared this delicious, easy way.

6 fillets cod or tilapia, thawed
   if frozen
1/2 c. onion, finely chopped
2 cloves garlic, minced
2 T. olive oil
2 T. fresh parsley, chopped

1 t. salt
1/8 t. pepper
6-oz. can frozen orange juice
   concentrate, thawed
1 T. lemon juice
Garnish: paprika, lemon slices

Arrange fish fillets in a lightly greased 13"x9" baking pan; set aside. In a small skillet, sauté onion and garlic in oil until tender. Stir in parsley, salt and pepper; spoon mixture over fish. Mix orange and lemon juices; drizzle over fish. Cover and bake at 400 degrees for 20 to 25 minutes, until fish flakes easily with a fork. Garnish with paprika and lemon slices. Serves 4 to 6.

Make frozen fish taste fresh and mild. Place the frozen fillets in a shallow dish, cover with milk and place them in the refrigerator to thaw overnight.

Dinners for the
Daily Dash

Fish Meets Chips

Sandra Sullivan
Aurora, CO

I love crispy fish but don't want to fry it...this is a tasty alternative.

4 c. potato chips, crushed
1/2 t. dried thyme
4 fillets cod, tilapia or perch,
    1/2 to 3/4 inch thick, thawed
    if frozen

2/3 c. honey-mustard salad
    dressing or mayonnaise

Mix crushed chips with thyme in a shallow dish; set aside. Pat fish fillets dry with paper towels. Brush both sides of fish with salad dressing or mayonnaise; coat fish on both sides with chip mixture. Arrange fish on an aluminum foil-lined baking sheet that has been sprayed with non-stick vegetable spray. Bake, uncovered, at 450 degrees for 6 to 10 minutes, until fish flakes easily with a fork. Serves 4.

Buttery sweet corn on the cob is so delicious in the summertime...why not enjoy it more often? Place 3 tablespoons melted butter in a microwave-safe dish, add 4 husked ears of corn and roll to coat. Cover with plastic wrap and microwave on high for 6 to 8 minutes.

Lattice Chicken Pot Pie

Beverley Williams
San Antonio, TX

This inexpensive dish was always a favorite at our house. My children loved it and their friends would always show up at dinnertime when they knew this was on the menu.

1 boneless, skinless chicken
    breast, cooked and cubed
4 c. frozen mixed vegetables,
    thawed
10-3/4 oz. can cream of chicken
    soup

10-3/4 oz. can cream of
    mushroom soup
1-1/2 t. dried rosemary
8-oz. tube refrigerated crescent
    rolls

In a large bowl, mix all ingredients except crescent rolls. Spoon into a lightly greased 13"x9" baking pan. Roll out crescent rolls without separating; pinch gently to close seams. Cut dough lengthwise into one-inch wide strips. Criss-cross strips over pan in a lattice pattern. Bake at 350 degrees for one to 1-1/2 hours, until bubbly and crust is golden. Makes 6 servings.

Comforting Chicken & Noodles

Marcie Fort
Shawnee, KS

I love to keep these ingredients on hand in case someone in the family comes down with the sniffles. It is instant and healthful "medicine"...sit back and enjoy!

2 32-oz. containers low-sodium
    chicken broth
12-oz. pkg. no-yolk broad egg
    noodles, uncooked
1 deli roast chicken, boned and
    shredded

2 10-3/4 oz. cans cream of
    mushroom soup
Optional: sour cream

Pour broth into a Dutch oven over medium-high heat; bring to a boil. Add noodles. Boil for 10 minutes, stirring occasionally; do not drain. Stir in chicken and soup; heat through. Serve in bowls, topped with sour cream, if desired. Makes 6 to 8 servings.

Dinners for the
Daily Dash

Herbed Chicken & Orzo

Eugenia Taylor
Stroudsburg, PA

A terrific hearty meal...wonderful when there isn't a lot of time to cook! My kids are great fans of this dish and request it often.

8-oz. pkg. orzo pasta, uncooked
14-1/2 oz. can cut green beans, drained
2 5.2-oz. pkgs. spreadable cream cheese with garlic & herbs
1/2 c. milk
1 deli roast chicken, cut into 6 serving-size pieces

Cook orzo according to package directions, adding green beans during last 3 minutes of cooking time; drain. In a large bowl, whisk together cream cheese and milk until blended. Add hot orzo mixture; stir until coated. Spoon into a greased 3-quart casserole dish. Top with chicken. Bake, covered, at 350 degrees for 30 to 40 minutes, until heated through. Let stand for 5 minutes. Serves 6.

Gena's Rice & Chicken Skillet

Becky Gentrup
Shakopee, MN

My best friend Gena gave me this recipe. I'm always on the lookout for quick one-dish recipes...my kids love it!

2 6.8-oz. pkgs. chicken-flavored rice vermicelli mix
4 to 6 boneless, skinless chicken breasts, cubed
1 T. canola oil
4 roma tomatoes, diced
1 c. finely shredded Cheddar cheese

Prepare rice as directed on package. Meanwhile, in a skillet over medium heat, cook chicken in oil until no longer pink in the center. Add chicken to rice. Sprinkle with tomatoes and cheese; let stand until cheese melts, about 5 minutes. Serves 4 to 6.

Sassy Sausage Jambalaya

Debra Elliott
Birmingham, AL

This quick & easy dish is a family favorite. I've added a few fresh vegetables to get my grandson Nicholas to eat his veggies.

3 T. butter
1 green pepper, diced
1 yellow pepper, diced
1 red pepper, diced
1 sweet onion, diced

1 to 2 tomatoes, diced
1 lb. smoked pork sausage,
  sliced into 1-inch rounds
8-1/2 oz. pkg. microwaveable
  Cajun rice & red beans

Add butter to a large skillet; melt over medium heat. Sauté peppers, onion and tomatoes for one to 2 minutes. Add sausage to skillet; heat through. Meanwhile, prepare rice in microwave according to package directions. Stir one cup cooked rice into mixture in skillet; reserve remaining rice for another meal. Simmer for 3 to 5 minutes to allow flavors to blend. Serves 4.

Add the words "You Are Special" around the rim of
a dinner plate with glass paint. Reserve it for family birthdays
and graduations...even for small accomplishments like a
child learning to tie her shoes. It's sure to become
a cherished tradition.

Dinners for the
Daily Dash

Spinach & Sausage Soup

Tamela James
Grove City, OH

This soup is a wonderful one-pot meal...it's one of my daughter Katie's favorites. Just add a basket of warm dinner rolls.

1 lb. ground Italian pork
   sausage
4 14-1/2 oz. cans chicken broth
0.7-oz. pkg. Italian salad
   dressing mix
8 new redskin potatoes,
   quartered and sliced

2 c. fresh baby spinach, or
   10-oz. pkg. frozen chopped
   spinach
Optional: grated Parmesan
   cheese

Brown sausage in a Dutch oven over medium-high heat; drain. Add broth, dressing mix and potatoes. Cook until potatoes are tender, about 10 minutes. Add spinach; reduce heat to low and simmer for 10 minutes. To serve, ladle into bowls; top with Parmesan cheese, if desired. Makes 8 to 10 servings.

Be a smart shopper. Make a shopping list, grouping items by the area of the store where they're found...produce, meats, canned goods and frozen foods. You'll breeze right down the aisles.

Butternut Veggie Soup

Samantha Reilly
Gig Harbor, WA

An easy way to use butternut squash without a lot of squash flavor, for those pickier eaters. Serve with biscuits or toast and butter.

1 butternut squash, peeled,
    seeded and cubed
2 c. cauliflower, cut into
    bite-size flowerets
1 T. olive oil
1 lb. ground beef
12 whole pearl onions,
    or 2 onions, chopped
28-oz. can crushed tomatoes

14-1/2 oz. can cut green beans,
    drained
11-oz. can corn, drained
4 c. water
3 T. beef soup base
3 T. fresh basil, chopped
2 T. fresh oregano, chopped
1 T. salt
1 t. pepper

Combine squash and cauliflower on a rimmed baking sheet; drizzle with oil. Bake, uncovered, at 350 degrees for about 30 minutes, until fork-tender; let cool. Meanwhile, brown beef with onions in a large soup pot over medium heat; drain. Add squash mixture, tomatoes with juice and remaining ingredients to soup pot. Simmer until heated through, stirring occasionally, about 10 to 15 minutes. Makes 8 to 10 servings.

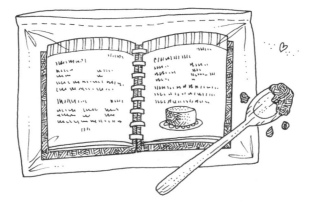

Keep a favorite cookbook clean and free of spatters. Slip it into a gallon-size plastic zipping bag before starting dinner.

Dinners for the
Daily Dash

Super-Easy Chicken Tortilla Soup

Bonnie Zeilenga
DeMotte, IN

A delicious, nutritious dinner that saves the day for busy moms!
I keep most of the ingredients for this snap-to-make soup on hand.
Then I pick up a rotisserie chicken on the way home from work, along
with a loaf of crusty bread and a bag of salad mix...simple!

1/2 c. onion, chopped
1 T. olive oil
14-1/2 oz. can diced tomatoes
10-3/4 oz. can reduced-fat
   cream of chicken soup
10-3/4 oz. can Cheddar cheese
   soup
10-1/2 oz. can chicken broth

10-oz. can red enchilada sauce
4-oz. can chopped green chiles
1 deli roast chicken, boned and
   shredded
Garnish: shredded sharp
   Mexican-blend or Cheddar
   cheese, sour cream, chopped
   fresh cilantro, tortilla strips

In a Dutch oven over medium heat, sauté onion in oil until tender and golden. Add remaining ingredients except garnish; stir. Bring to a boil; reduce heat to medium-low. Cover and simmer for one hour, stirring occasionally. May also be prepared in a slow cooker; cover and cook on high setting for 2 hours. At serving time, ladle into soup bowls; add desired toppings. Makes 8 servings.

Make your own savory chicken broth. After slicing
the meat from a deli chicken, cover the bones with water in
a stockpot. Onion and celery trimmings can be added too.
Simmer gently for 30 to 40 minutes, then strain and
refrigerate in recipe-size containers.

Veggieful Italian Hot Dish

Amanda Walton
Marysville, OH

*The kids never guess how many veggies are hidden
in this sausage & pasta dish...I love it!*

16-oz. pkg. rotini pasta,
  uncooked
1 red onion, chopped
1 green, red or yellow pepper,
  chopped
2 to 3 t. olive oil
1 c. cauliflower, chopped

1 c. broccoli, chopped
24-oz. jar pasta sauce
14-1/2 oz. can diced tomatoes
1 lb. mild Italian ground
  pork sausage
Garnish: shredded Parmesan
  cheese

Cook pasta according to package directions, just until tender; drain.
Meanwhile, in a large skillet over medium heat, sauté onion and
pepper in olive oil for about 5 minutes. Add cauliflower and broccoli;
cook until vegetables are tender. Add sausage and cook until browned;
drain. Stir in pasta sauce and tomatoes with juice. Reduce heat to
medium-low and simmer for 5 minutes. Add cooked pasta to skillet;
stir gently and simmer another 5 minutes. Serve sprinkled with
Parmesan cheese. Serves 6.

A flexible plastic cutting mat makes speedy work
of slicing & dicing...after chopping, just fold it in half
and pour ingredients into the mixing bowl.

Dinners for the
Daily Dash

Cheesy Hashbrowns & Beef
Amanda Gladden
Oneonta, AL

A favorite comfort-food meal for my kids and myself.

1 lb. ground beef
1/2 c. onion, chopped
1/2 c. green pepper, chopped
2 T. oil
2 to 3 potatoes, peeled and diced

seasoned salt to taste
10-oz. can diced tomatoes with
green chiles
1 c. shredded Cheddar cheese

In a large skillet over medium heat, combine beef, onion and green pepper. Cook until beef is browned and onion is tender; drain. Meanwhile, heat oil in a separate skillet. Cook potatoes until tender and golden; season with salt. Add potatoes and tomatoes with juice to beef mixture. Cook for 5 to 10 minutes, stirring occasionally. Remove from heat; top with cheese. Cover and let stand until cheese melts, about 5 minutes. Makes 4 servings.

Oops, the family's dinner plans have changed, but you've already put out food to thaw. No problem! As long as some ice crystals remain, it's perfectly safe to return partially defrosted food to the freezer.

Garden Sloppy Joes

Analysa Larsen
Salt Lake City, UT

A great way to use fresh produce...even my kids eat this up!

1 lb. ground beef
1 c. onion, chopped
1 green pepper, finely diced
2 carrots, peeled and grated
1 tomato, diced
1 tomato, puréed
3 T. brown sugar, packed

3 T. catsup
2 T. Worcestershire sauce
1 T. garlic salt
1 t. balsamic vinegar
10 whole-wheat hamburger
  buns, split and toasted

In a large soup pot over medium heat, brown beef with onion, pepper and carrots; drain. Stir in remaining ingredients except buns. Bring to a boil; reduce heat to medium-low. Cover and simmer for 30 minutes, stirring occasionally. Using a slotted spoon, scoop onto toasted buns. Makes 10 servings.

No more flimsy paper plates at the next potluck...they'll fit nice and snug inside a plastic flying disc. After lunch, it makes a terrific gift for everyone to take home!

Dinners for the
Daily Dash

Greek Meatball Pitas

Jenn Erickson
Pacific Grove, CA

When my daughter Mackenzie was a toddler, her favorite food was spinach. I had a hunch that she'd follow in her older sister Madeleine's footsteps and start getting more finicky as she got older, so I decided to create as many moments for her to "bond" with spinach as possible. These meatballs are quickly devoured by kids and grown-ups alike...they pack well in lunchboxes too!

1 T. butter
1 T. plus 1 t. extra-virgin olive
  oil, divided
1/2 c. red onion, diced
2 cloves garlic, minced
10-oz. pkg. frozen spinach,
  thawed and well-drained
1 t. dried oregano
1 to 1-1/3 lbs. ground turkey
  breast

4-oz. container crumbled
  feta cheese
2 t. salt
4 to 6 pita rounds, halved, split
  and warmed
Garnish: chopped lettuce,
  tomatoes, cucumber and
  Kalamata olives, thinly sliced
  red onion

Heat a large non-stick skillet over medium heat; melt butter with one tablespoon oil. Add onion and garlic; cook for 5 minutes. Transfer mixture to a large bowl and let cool; stir in spinach and oregano. Add uncooked turkey, cheese, salt and remaining oil. Mix well; form into 20 bite-size meatballs. Add meatballs to skillet over medium-high heat. Cook for 8 to 10 minutes, tossing occasionally, until lightly golden and cooked through. To serve, fill each warm pita with several meatballs, desired toppings and a dollop of Tzatziki Sauce; fold taco-style. Serves 4 to 6.

Tzatziki Sauce:

1/3 c. cucumber, chopped
1 clove garlic, minced
1-1/2 to 2 c. Greek yogurt

juice of 1/2 lemon
1 t. dried oregano
salt and pepper to taste

Combine all ingredients in a food processor; process until smooth.

Balsamic Chicken & Penne

Mary Nehring
Belmont, NC

I like fresh asparagus in this recipe, but my kids don't care for it, so sometimes I substitute fresh green beans...they'll eat those!

1/2 c. extra-virgin olive oil
1/4 c. balsamic vinegar
2 T. country Dijon mustard
2 T. sugar
3 cloves garlic, minced
1/2 t. salt
1/4 t. cayenne pepper, or to taste
4 boneless, skinless chicken
    breasts

8-oz. pkg. whole-wheat penne
    pasta, uncooked
1 bunch asparagus, trimmed,
    chopped and steamed
Optional: shredded Parmesan
    cheese

In a large plastic zipping bag, combine olive oil, balsamic vinegar, mustard, sugar, garlic and seasonings. Squeeze bag to mix well. Add chicken to bag; turn to coat. Seal bag and refrigerate at least 4 hours to overnight, turning bag occasionally. When ready to prepare chicken, drain marinade into a saucepan; heat to boiling for 15 minutes. Meanwhile, cook pasta according to package directions; drain. Broil chicken until chicken juices run clear, about 12 to 15 minutes. Cut chicken into bite-size pieces. To serve, combine chicken, marinade, asparagus and pasta. Toss to coat. Serve with Parmesan cheese, if desired. Makes 8 servings.

Take advantage of sales at the meat counter! Freeze uncooked chicken, beef or pork cutlets with marinade in freezer bags. After thawing overnight in the fridge, meat can go right into the skillet or under the broiler for a savory meal.

Dinners for the
Daily Dash

Mooncha's Chicken Chow Mein
Susan Jacobs
Vista, CA

The original recipe came from my Korean aunt by marriage in 1967, and I later adapted it to fit my family's tastes. Any leftovers are great for lunch the next day, but a warning...I've found this recipe doesn't go as far with teenagers in the house as it once did with small kids!

3-1/2 lbs. chicken
3 c. long-cooking rice, uncooked
1-1/2 c. celery, sliced
1 c. carrots, peeled and chopped
1 c. onion, chopped

1/4 to 1/2 c. soy sauce
pepper to taste
Optional: 15-oz. can bean
   sprouts, drained
Garnish: additional soy sauce

In a large stockpot, cover chicken with water. Simmer over medium-low heat for about one hour, until chicken is very tender. Remove chicken from stockpot, reserving broth. Let chicken cool. Stir rice into broth in stockpot; simmer for about 10 minutes. Add celery, carrots and onion to stockpot. Continue to simmer for about 10 minutes, until rice and vegetables are tender. Add a little more water if necessary to finish cooking rice; mixture should not be soupy. Shred chicken into bite-size pieces, discarding skin and bones. Stir chicken into rice mixture along with soy sauce, pepper and bean sprouts, if using. Serve in bowls with additional soy sauce on the side. Makes 10 servings.

After a simple dinner, a sweet & simple dessert is in order. Place scoops of sherbet in parfait glasses and slip a fortune cookie over the edge of each glass. Be sure to have everyone share their fortunes!

Tina's Simple Shepherd's Pie
Tina Goodpasture
Meadowview, VA

I love this dish...it's easy and delicious to make. I use real potatoes for that homemade taste, but you can certainly use instant. Add a skillet of buttery cornbread for a delicious country dinner.

2 T. extra-virgin olive oil
1 c. carrots, peeled and chopped
1 c. pearl onions
1 lb. lean ground turkey
1 T. all-purpose flour
3/4 c. low-sodium chicken broth
1 c. frozen peas
2-1/2 t. fresh rosemary, chopped
salt and pepper to taste
3 c. mashed potatoes

In a large saucepan, heat olive oil over medium heat. Add carrots and onions; cook until soft, about 5 minutes. Add turkey and cook until browned, about 6 minutes; break up turkey with a wooden spoon. Stir in broth, peas and rosemary; season with salt and pepper. Bring to a simmer. Cook until slightly thickened, about 5 minutes. Season with more salt and pepper, if desired. Spoon mixture into an ungreased 9" deep-dish pie plate. Spread mashed potatoes over top. Bake, uncovered, at 400 degrees for about 25 minutes, until heated through and golden. Makes 8 servings.

Another terrific way to serve mashed potatoes...scoop them into a bowl and top with hot gravy, chopped turkey and corn for a homestyle dinner-in-a-bowl.

Dinners for the
Daily Dash

Savory Chicken & Rice Soup
Lisa Pettigrew
Brentwood, TN

I remember going to visit Grandma and smelling this soup cooking in her kitchen...so yummy! It's always welcome in soup weather and for anyone who's not feeling well.

1 T. extra-virgin olive oil
1 onion, chopped
2 cloves garlic, minced
2 carrots, peeled and sliced
    1/2-inch thick on the
    diagonal
2 stalks celery, halved
    lengthwise and sliced
    1/2-inch thick

4 sprigs fresh thyme
1 bay leaf
8 c. regular or low-sodium
    chicken broth
1 c. water
1 c. long-cooking rice, uncooked
1-1/2 c. cooked chicken breasts,
    shredded
salt and pepper to taste

Heat olive oil in a soup pot over medium heat. Add onion, garlic, carrots, celery and herbs. Cook and stir for about 6 minutes, until vegetables are softened but not browned. Add broth and water; bring to a boil. Stir in rice and chicken; season with salt and pepper. Reduce heat to medium-low. Cover and simmer until rice is tender, about 30 minutes. Discard bay leaf before serving. Makes 6 to 8 servings.

A soup supper is warm and comforting on a chilly night... it's so easy to prepare too. Just add a basket of muffins and a crock of sweet butter. Dinner is served!

111

Mexican Chicken Casserole

Kim Wilson
Melbourne, FL

*One day I needed to find a recipe that eleven children and
four adults would like...this casserole fit the bill. It's so good!*

1 onion, chopped
1 red pepper, chopped
1 poblano pepper, chopped,
   or 4-oz. can diced green
   chiles
1 T. oil
1 c. chicken broth
1/4 c. all-purpose flour
1 t. ground cumin
2 c. half-and-half

8-oz. pkg. reduced-fat cream
   cheese, cubed
2 10-oz. cans diced tomatoes
   with green chiles
1/4 c. fresh cilantro, chopped
15 corn tortillas, halved
4 boneless, skinless chicken
   breasts, cooked and cubed
3 c. shredded Colby Jack cheese

In a large saucepan over medium heat, sauté onion and peppers in oil,
just until soft, about 4 minutes. Add broth; whisk in flour and cumin
until smooth. Add half-and-half and cream cheese. Reduce heat to
medium-low. Simmer until sauce thickens, whisking often. Stir in
tomatoes and cilantro; remove from heat and set side. In a greased
deep 13"x9" baking pan, layer 1/3 of tortillas; layer with 1/3 of cheese
and half of chicken. Repeat layers, ending with a tortilla on top. Spoon
sauce over all; top with remaining cheese. Bake, uncovered, at
375 degrees for 35 to 40 minutes, until bubbly and cheese is melted.
Makes 8 servings.

"Fried" ice cream is a special ending
to a south-of-the-border meal. Scoop
balls of vanilla ice cream, roll them in
crushed sugar-coated corn flake cereal
and return to the freezer. Serve
garnished with a drizzle of honey
and a dollop of whipped cream...
scrumptious!

Dinners for the
Daily Dash

Southwestern Chicken Chili

Laura Witham
Anchorage, AK

*My husband and I are trying to eat healthier and save money...
a challenge that's been quite fun and delicious! I tossed together this
recipe as I was hurrying to get supper on the table before I headed
out the door. We liked it so much, I wrote down the recipe to share
with my friends.*

2 T. extra-virgin olive oil
1 to 2 boneless, skinless chicken
   breasts, diced
1 yellow onion, diced
2 cloves garlic, diced
1/8 t. salt
14-1/2 oz. can fire-roasted
   diced tomatoes
11-oz. can corn, drained

15-oz. can black beans, drained
   and rinsed
1 T. Worcestershire sauce
1 t. Italian seasoning
salt and pepper to taste
Optional: regular or fat-free sour
   cream, shredded Cheddar
   cheese

Heat oil in a skillet over medium-high heat; add chicken and cook until
golden. Add onion, garlic and salt; reduce heat to medium-low. Add
tomatoes with juice, corn, beans, Worcestershire sauce and seasoning.
Bring to a simmer; reduce heat to low. Cover and cook for 15 minutes,
stirring frequently. Season with salt and pepper. Serve garnished as
desired. Makes 4 servings.

Crunchy toppings can really add fun and flavor to soup or
chili. Some fun choices...fish-shaped crackers, bacon bits,
French fried onions, sunflower seeds or toasted nuts.

Baked Pasta e Fagioli

Ashley Billings
Shamong, NJ

This twist on an Italian classic is a filling and budget-friendly meatless meal that everyone loves. It's a recipe I turn to whenever I need to easily feed a crowd!

8-oz. pkg. whole-wheat penne
    pasta, uncooked
1 T. olive oil
1/2 onion, chopped
1 stalk celery, chopped
2 cloves garlic, minced
1 c. chicken broth
16-oz. can reduced-sodium dark
    red kidney beans, drained

16-oz. can reduced-sodium
    pinto beans, drained
1 tomato, chopped
pepper to taste
10-oz. pkg. frozen chopped
    spinach, thawed and drained
1/2 c. favorite shredded cheese,
    divided

Cook pasta according to package directions, just until tender. Drain pasta, reserving 1/4 cup cooking water; return pasta to pot. Meanwhile, heat olive oil in a skillet over medium heat. Add onion and celery; cook for 9 to 10 minutes, stirring often. Add garlic; cook for one minute. Stir in broth, beans, tomato and pepper; heat to boiling. Reduce heat to medium-low; stir in spinach and heat through. To pasta in pot, add reserved pasta water, skillet mixture and 1/4 cup cheese; toss until mixed. Transfer to a greased 13"x9" baking pan; top with remaining cheese. Bake, uncovered, at 400 degrees for 15 to 20 minutes, until bubbly and golden. Serves 6.

For a side dish that practically cooks itself, fill aluminum foil packets with sliced fresh veggies. Top with seasoning salt and 2 ice cubes, seal and bake at 450 degrees for 20 to 25 minutes. Delicious...and the kids can help fix the packets.

Dinners for the
Daily Dash

3-Cheese Stuffed Shells

Sharon Laney
Maryville, TN

This is a favorite easy meal for my family.

12-oz. pkg. jumbo pasta shells,
    uncooked
28-oz. jar favorite spaghetti
    sauce, divided
8-oz. pkg. shredded mozzarella
    cheese
8-oz. container ricotta cheese
1/2 c. grated Parmesan cheese

1 egg, beaten
1 T. dried parsley
Optional: 10-oz. pkg. frozen
    chopped spinach, thawed
    and well-drained
Optional: additional shredded
    mozzarella cheese

Cook pasta shells according to package directions; drain. Meanwhile, spread half of sauce in the bottom of a lightly greased 11"x9" baking pan; set aside. In a bowl, combine cheeses, egg, parsley and spinach, if using; mix well. Spoon cheese mixture into shells. Arrange stuffed shells in pan in a single layer; cover with remaining sauce. If desired, top with more cheese. Bake, uncovered, at 350 degrees for about one hour, until hot and bubbly. Makes 10 servings.

Making stuffed shells for supper? Instead of a spoon, combine ingredients in a plastic zipping bag instead of a bowl. Blend by squeezing the bag, snip off a corner and pipe the filling into the shells...no muss, no fuss!

Kathy's Italian Zucchini Dish
Kathleen Whitsett
Greenwood, IN

It always amazes me how much zucchini can be produced by two little plants! I came up with this recipe as a kid-friendly meatless dish. It is very simple, healthy and fast to fix. The colors of the dish and the yellow saffron rice are so pretty together. My family loves it, my zucchini never goes to waste and it freezes well too.

1 T. butter
1 T. olive oil
1 sweet onion, sliced and
    separated into rings
1 to 2 zucchini, sliced
14-1/2 oz. can diced tomatoes
    with garlic and basil

1/2 t. dried basil
1/2 t. dried oregano
salt and pepper to taste
1-1/2 c. grated Parmesan
    cheese, divided
8-oz. pkg. saffron rice mix,
    cooked

In a large skillet over medium heat, melt butter with olive oil. Add onion; cook until soft and golden, about 6 to 8 minutes. Add zucchini; cook until zucchini softens, about 5 to 7 minutes. Reduce heat to low; stir in tomatoes with juice and seasonings. Simmer for 15 to 20 minutes, stirring occasionally. Just before serving, stir in one cup Parmesan cheese. Serve zucchini mixture over cooked rice; top with remaining Parmesan cheese. Makes 5 to 6 servings.

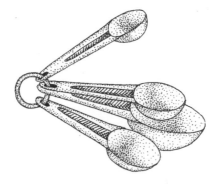

Pick up an extra set of measuring spoons for speedy meal prep...you'll never need to stop in the middle of a recipe to wash spoons!

Dinners for the
Daily Dash

Prize-Winning Chilighetti

Betsy Smith
McKinney, TX

Back in 1968, my mother was selected as "Cook of the Month" for this recipe by a Jackson, Mississippi newspaper. You'll love it too...this is probably my most-requested recipe of all time!

16-oz. pkg vermicelli pasta, uncooked
1-1/2 lbs. ground beef
salt, pepper and garlic powder to taste
1 onion, chopped
15-oz. can chili without beans

14-1/2 oz. can diced tomatoes
6-oz. jar sliced mushrooms
8-oz. container sour cream
1-1/2 c. shredded Cheddar cheese
Garnish: grated Parmesan cheese

Cook pasta according to package directions, just until tender. Drain and return to cooking pot. Meanwhile, brown beef in a skillet over medium heat; drain. Season beef with salt, pepper and garlic powder; set aside in a bowl. Add onion to skillet; sauté until golden. Return beef to skillet; stir in chili and undrained tomatoes and mushrooms. Heat through. Add beef mixture to pasta; stir gently. Fold in sour cream and Cheddar cheese. Transfer mixture to a greased 13"x9" baking pan; sprinkle with Parmesan cheese. Bake, uncovered, at 350 degrees for 45 minutes, or until hot and bubbly. Makes 10 to 12 servings.

Turn leftover spaghetti into tasty noodle patties. Mix 2 to 3 cups cold, cooked pasta with 2 beaten eggs and 1/2 cup ricotta cheese; form into 4 patties. Cook in a skillet in a little oil until golden, 3 to 4 minutes per side. Serve topped with warm spaghetti sauce or a sprinkle of Parmesan.

Upside-Down Salami Pizza

Barb Rudyk
Vermilion, Alberta

This pizza is very easy to assemble...budget-friendly too.
You can add any pizza toppings and spices you like.

1 t. butter
3/4 lb. deli salami, cut into strips
1 yellow onion, chopped
1/2 c. green pepper, chopped
1 c. sliced mushrooms
15-oz. can tomato sauce
1 t. dried oregano

1 c. shredded mozzarella cheese
2 eggs, beaten
1 c. milk
1 T. oil
1 c. all-purpose flour
1/4 t. salt
2 T. shredded Parmesan cheese

Melt butter in an oven-safe skillet over medium heat. Sauté salami, onion, green pepper and mushrooms until tender. Drain; stir in tomato sauce and oregano. Spread salami mixture evenly in skillet. If skillet is not oven-safe, transfer mixture to a greased 9"x9" baking pan. Sprinkle with mozzarella cheese; set aside. In a bowl, whisk together eggs, milk and oil until well blended. Add flour and salt; beat until smooth. Pour egg mixture evenly over salami mixture in pan. Sprinkle with Parmesan cheese. Bake, uncovered, at 350 degrees for 25 to 30 minutes, until puffed and golden. Invert pizza onto a serving platter; cut into wedges or squares. Makes 6 servings.

Keep a big roll of wide white freezer paper on hand for casual get-togethers...party tables can be covered in a snap and the paper can be tossed out afterwards.

Dinners for the
Daily Dash

Stuffed Peppers with Feta

Lyuba Brooke
Jacksonville, FL

My whole family, including my 22-month-old,
absolutely loves these peppers!

2 T. oil
2 cloves garlic
1/2 c. onion, chopped
1 lb. ground beef
1/2 lb. ground pork
2 T. fresh parsley, minced
1/2 t. dried marjoram

1/2 t. dried rosemary
salt and pepper to taste
8-oz. can tomato sauce
2 c. cooked orzo pasta
4 green peppers, tops cut off
1/2 c. crumbled feta cheese

Heat oil in a large skillet over medium heat. Add garlic; sauté until fragrant, one to 2 minutes. Add onion; cook until transparent. Mix together beef and pork; crumble into skillet. When meat is nearly browned, add parsley, seasonings and tomato sauce. When meat is browned, add cooked pasta and mix well; remove from heat. Spoon meat mixture into peppers, filling generously. Arrange peppers in a greased 2-quart casserole dish; top with cheese. Cover with aluminum foil. Bake at 350 degrees for 25 to 30 minutes, until hot and bubbly. Makes 4 servings.

Turn fruit juice into a special-occasion beverage...add a splash of ginger ale and a skewer of fruit cubes lined up on a plastic straw.

Take-It-Easy Tortellini Soup

Danielle Dorward
San Diego, CA

This easy, creamy soup is so versatile and filling. My five-year-old daughter Annalise always asks for a second helping. Homemade sauce adds great flavor, but your favorite jar sauce works, too!

1/2 lb. ground beef
1/2 onion, diced
3 cloves garlic, minced
1 to 2 T. olive oil
1 carrot, peeled and minced
5 c. spaghetti sauce
8-oz. pkg. cream cheese, room temperature and cubed
4 c. chicken broth

1-1/2 c. zucchini, shredded
5-oz. pkg. fresh baby spinach
1/2 c. sliced cremini or button mushrooms
19-oz. pkg. refrigerated cheese-filled tortellini, uncooked
pepper to taste
Garnish: shredded Parmesan cheese

In a large stockpot over medium heat, brown beef, onion and garlic in olive oil. Drain; add carrot and cook another 2 minutes. Stir in sauce. Use a whisk to stir in cream cheese until smooth. Add broth; bring to a boil. Reduce heat to medium-low; simmer for about 10 minutes, stirring occasionally. Add zucchini, spinach, mushrooms and tortellini. Simmer for 7 to 9 more minutes, just until tortellini is warmed through and tender. Season with pepper. Serve soup topped with Parmesan cheese. Makes 4 to 6 servings.

It's a lovely thing...everyone sitting down together, sharing food.

–Alice May Brock

Dinners for the
Daily Dash

Inside-Out Ravioli

Lisa Harrell
Rural Hall, NC

When I was in college, I used to make this meal once a week. Mom was working and I took care of my little brother Johnny, who is 12 years younger than me. He would help me mix everything and put it into the casserole dish. When Mom got home and complimented us on how good dinner smelled, Johnny was so proud! It felt good to have her come home to a home-cooked meal after she'd worked so hard to make ends meet. Now this dish is a favorite with my own three kids...and a great way to hide the spinach!

16-oz. pkg. small shell pasta, uncooked
1 lb. ground beef
1 c. onion, chopped
8-oz. pkg. sliced mushrooms
8-oz. pkg. frozen chopped spinach, thawed and drained
1 egg, beaten
1/2 c. dry bread crumbs
1 t. salt
1 t. pepper
1 t. Italian seasoning
16-oz. jar spaghetti sauce
1 c. shredded mozzarella cheese
Garnish: grated Parmesan cheese

Cook pasta according to package directions; drain and set aside. Meanwhile, in a skillet over medium heat, brown beef with onion; drain. In a large bowl, combine cooked pasta, beef mixture and remaining ingredients except sauce and cheeses. Transfer mixture to a greased 13"x9" baking pan. Top with sauce and mozzarella cheese. Bake, uncovered, at 350 degrees for 45 minutes, or until hot and bubbly. Sprinkle with Parmesan cheese at serving time. Makes 10 servings.

Frozen veggies come in so many colorful, delicious blends...and they're almost as good as homegrown. Add variety to favorite recipes or toss with dried herbs and crispy bacon for a quick side.

Mexican Stir-Fried Rice

John Newsome
Columbia, SC

This is definitely a family favorite, created one day from what we could find in our pantry! Now we come back to this recipe time & time again because it is delicious and budget-friendly.

1-1/2 c. long-cooking brown
   rice, uncooked
3 T. olive oil
10-oz. can chicken breast,
   drained
2 cloves garlic, minced
15-oz. can black beans, drained
   and rinsed

1 sweet potato, peeled and diced
1 tomato, diced
3 to 4 T. favorite salsa
2 t. chili powder, or more
   to taste

Cook rice according to package directions; drain and rinse. Spread rice on a large plate and place in refrigerator to cool. Heat oil over medium-high heat in a large skillet. Add chicken; shred with a fork and stir until warmed through. Add garlic; sauté for 30 seconds. Stir in beans; heat through. Stir in sweet potato and tomato; add cooked rice. Cook, stirring constantly and scraping bottom of skillet until well mixed. If necessary, add a little more oil to keep rice from sticking. Stir in salsa and chili powder. Makes 6 to 8 servings.

Make clean-up a snap! Before dinner even starts,
fill the sink with hot, soapy water. Put dishes right in
when cooking's finished and, by the time dinner and
dessert are eaten, they'll be a breeze to wash clean.

Dinners for the *Daily Dash*

White Chicken Chili

Janelle DeWitt
Grant, IA

When any of my kids or grandkids get sick, they call and ask me to make this chili for them. Guaranteed to make them feel better!

3 15-oz. cans Great Northern
   beans
5 c. cooked chicken, diced
   or shredded
32-oz. container chicken broth
16-oz. jar salsa
8-oz. pkg. shredded Pepper Jack
   cheese

2 cloves garlic, minced
2 t. ground cumin
pepper to taste
Optional: 1/2 c. corn chips,
   finely crushed
Garnish: additional shredded
   cheese, sour cream,
   corn chips

In a soup pot, combine undrained beans and remaining ingredients except corn chips and garnish. Cook over medium-high heat for about 30 minutes, stirring occasionally, until heated through and cheese is melted. If a thicker chili is desired, stir in crushed corn chips and simmer for 10 minutes. Garnish bowls of chili as desired. Makes 12 servings.

Hollow out round crusty loaves for bread bowls...
they make soup even tastier! For small kids,
dinner rolls are the perfect size.

Best Chicken & Dumplings

Jessica Kraus
Delaware, OH

What's more comforting than a bowl of made-from-scratch chicken & dumplings? The key to this recipe is lots of flour. Make sure you flour everything, including the table you are using and the rolling pin... it will make the dumpling sauce come out oh-so creamy!

2 c. all-purpose flour
1/2 t. baking powder
1/8 t. salt
2 T. butter

1 c. milk
8 c. chicken broth
3 c. cooked chicken, cubed

In a bowl, combine flour, baking powder and salt. Cut in butter with a fork. Stir in milk until dough forms a ball. Sprinkle a work surface generously with flour. Roll out dough thinly with a very well-floured rolling pin. With a floured pizza cutter, cut dough into one-inch squares. With a floured fork, lift dumplings off the table and onto a floured plate. Pour broth into a large saucepan; bring to a boil over medium-high heat. Drop in dumplings, one at a time, stirring while you add them. Add any extra flour from the plate into the broth as well, to help thicken the sauce. Boil dumplings for about 15 to 20 minutes, until no longer doughy tasting. Add chicken and heat through, about 5 minutes. Serve chicken, dumplings and broth in bowls. Makes 8 servings.

Save time when cooking...tuck a measuring cup into each of your countertop canisters. They'll be ready to scoop out flour and sugar when you need them.

Dinners for the
Daily Dash

Comfort Potato & Ham Soup

Amy Gordon
Pine River, MN

I often make this soup a couple days after Christmas, it's a great way to use up leftover ham. My four kids love to help! I add the onion while the kids aren't looking. Just remember to add some love too. I like to serve it with different kinds of breads and rolls from my **Gooseberry Patch** *cookbooks.*

8 c. water
5 cubes chicken bouillon
6 to 8 potatoes, peeled and
    cut into 1/2-inch cubes
2 to 3 carrots, peeled and sliced
1/2 c. onion, minced
2 stalks celery, sliced
2 to 3 c. cooked ham, diced

1-1/2 t. garlic salt
1-1/2 t. salt
1-1/2 t. pepper
1 c. instant mashed potato
    flakes
1/4 c. butter, sliced
5-oz. can evaporated milk
1/2 c. grated Parmesan cheese

In a large soup pot over medium-high heat, combine water, bouillon cubes, vegetables, ham and seasonings. Bring to a boil. Reduce heat to medium; simmer until potatoes are tender, about 15 to 20 minutes, stirring occasionally. Shortly before serving time, stir in remaining ingredients; simmer for 10 minutes, until thickened. Makes 8 to 10 servings.

If you have an overabundance of fresh veggies from
the garden or farmers' market, save them by cooking up
a big pot of soup and freezing it in family-size portions.

Sam's Chicken-Cabbage Soup

Tiffani Schulte
Wyandotte, MI

My son Sam is not a big soup eater, but one chilly day I had a cabbage to use up and decided to concoct a new soup recipe. The result has become one of his most-requested meals...and it could not be faster to toss together! It freezes beautifully as well.

1 T. butter
1 T. olive oil
1 onion, diced
1 green or red pepper, diced
2 to 3 cloves garlic, minced
1 jalapeño pepper, seeds
    removed and minced
1 lb. ground chicken
28-oz. can whole plum tomatoes

2 14-1/2 oz. cans chicken broth
4 to 6 c. water
2 to 4 t. chicken bouillon
    granules, to taste
1 to 2 t. seasoned salt, to taste
pepper to taste
1 head cabbage, coarsely
    shredded

In a large soup pot, melt butter with olive oil over medium heat. Cook onion for about 3 to 4 minutes. Add green or red pepper; continue cooking until soft. Add garlic and jalapeño pepper; continue cooking and stirring for one to 2 minutes. Add chicken and cook, breaking up with a spoon, until no longer pink. Add tomatoes with juice, breaking up tomatoes as you add them. Add remaining ingredients except cabbage; mix well. Stir in cabbage. Reduce heat to medium-low. Cook until cabbage is tender and has cooked down, about 20 minutes, stirring occasionally. Makes 10 servings.

Make-ahead freezer meals are real life-savers! Set aside
a weekend each month to prepare several family-pleasing
dishes to tuck in the freezer. Why not invite a friend to help?
You can both be filling your freezers while you
get caught up on the latest news.

Dinners for the
Daily Dash

Favorite Vegetable-Beef Soup

Judy Taylor
Butler, MO

I lost my mother when I was young, but I will always remember this wonderful soup that she made. She did not use a recipe, but I have been able to duplicate it through practice. My family loves it just as I did when I was growing up. This delicious soup can be made ahead of time and freezes well.

1 lb. stew beef cubes
1 onion, diced
1/4 c. margarine
1 c. water
6 potatoes, peeled and cut into
   1/2-inch cubes
1 lb. carrots, peeled and sliced
   1/2-inch thick

4 stalks celery, sliced 1/2-inch
   thick
salt and pepper to taste
46-oz. can cocktail vegetable
   juice or tomato juice
1 head cabbage, cut into large
   chunks
2 to 3 bay leaves

In a large pot over medium-high heat, brown beef and onion in margarine. Add water, potatoes, carrots, celery, salt and pepper. Reduce heat to medium-low. Cook until tender, about 30 minutes. Stir in vegetable juice and cabbage; add bay leaves on top. Cover and cook over low heat for 2 hours, stirring occasionally. Remove bay leaves at serving time. Makes 6 to 8 servings.

Kids are sure to know the old tale of Stone Soup...why not let it inspire a chilly-weather get-together? Invite everyone to bring a favorite veggie, while you provide a bubbling stockpot of broth. While the soup simmers, you can play board games or just chat for an old-fashioned good time.

Mom's Best Chili

Lynnette Jones
East Flat Rock, NC

My family enjoys this chili recipe better than any other! It needs to simmer for awhile, but the results are worth it. I like to double the recipe and freeze half of it for later.

3/4 lb. ground beef round
   or sirloin
1 onion, finely chopped
1 T. chili powder
1 t. salt
1 t. pepper

15-oz. can kidney beans,
   drained
15-oz. can ranch style beans
11-1/2 oz. can tomato juice
8-oz. can tomato sauce

Brown beef in a Dutch oven over medium heat. Add onion; cover and cook for 5 to 7 minutes, until onion is tender. Drain; stir in seasonings. Cook for 2 to 3 minutes. Add remaining ingredients; mix well. Reduce heat to low; cover and simmer for 2 to 3 hours, stirring occasionally. Makes 8 to 10 servings.

A fun and simple meal...try a chili dog bar! Along with cooked hot dogs and buns, set out some chili, shredded cheese, sauerkraut, chopped onions and your favorite condiments. Kids love it, and it's a terrific way to use leftover chili.

Dinners for the
Daily Dash

Sloppy Joes From Scratch

*Lynn Gauthier
Midland, MI*

When my sister-in-law Laure served these Sloppy Joes from slow cookers at her son Matt's wedding rehearsal dinner, all of the guests wanted the recipe. I've shared it so many times...everyone just loves them! It tastes even better the next day.

1-1/2 lbs. ground beef	2 T. all-purpose flour
2 T. green pepper, diced	2 T. brown sugar, packed,
2 T. dried, minced onion	or more to taste
1/4 t. celery flakes	1 T. vinegar
1 c. catsup	1 T. mustard
1/2 t. salt	10 to 12 hamburger buns or
1/4 t. pepper	onion buns, split

Brown beef in a large skillet over medium heat; drain. Add green pepper, onion and celery flakes; simmer until tender. Stir in remaining ingredients except buns. Simmer over medium-low heat for about 30 minutes, stirring occasionally. Add a little more brown sugar to offset vinegar, if needed. Serve on buns. Makes 10 to 12 servings.

Set out stacks of colorful bandannas...they make super-size fun napkins when enjoying Sloppy Joes!

Ready When You Are!

Mom's Strombolis

Michelle Johnson
Drexel Hill, PA

I used to help my mom make these as a kid. I got to sprinkle the flour and roll the dough. Now I make them and my kids help me! I am always asked to make these for friends' parties...they are a huge hit.

1 loaf frozen bread or pizza
   dough, thawed
1/2 c. all-purpose flour
1/4 to 1/2 lb. deli sharp Cooper
   or pasteurized process
   cheese, sliced and divided

1/4 lb. sliced pepperoni, sliced
1/4 lb. sliced deli capicallo
   hot spicy ham

Sprinkle dough and work surface with flour. Shape dough into a ball; roll out into a 14-inch circle with a floured rolling pin. Leaving a 1/2-inch border around the edges, layer dough with most of the cheese slices. Add all of the pepperoni and capicallo ham. Top with reserved cheese slices. Roll up jelly-roll style; pinch sides and ends together. Place on a lightly greased baking sheet. Bake at 350 degrees for 30 to 40 minutes, until golden. Remove from oven; let cool for 10 minutes before slicing. Baked stromboli may be cooled, wrapped in aluminum foil and frozen. To reheat if frozen, bake in foil at 350 degrees for 20 minutes; open up foil and bake for an additional 10 minutes. Makes 12 to 15 servings.

If busy kids can't get home for dinner, take it to them!
Pack a tailgating basket and enjoy picnicking with them at
the ballpark. Be sure to pack extra for hungry team members.

Saucy Beef Enchiladas

Liz Kelsay
Whiteland, IN

One of my husband's favorite dinners! I usually double the recipe, serve one pan and freeze the other...a perfect meal for a busy night. You can adjust the spiciness by changing up the salsa.

1 lb. ground beef
1-1/4 oz. pkg. taco seasoning
   mix
1/2 c. water
16-oz. can refried beans
16-oz. jar salsa

2 10-3/4 oz. cans cream of
   chicken soup
1-1/2 c. milk
10 8-inch flour tortillas
2 c. shredded Mexican-blend
   cheese

Brown beef in a large skillet over medium heat; drain. Stir in taco seasoning and water; bring to a boil. Reduce heat to low. Simmer, uncovered, for 15 to 20 minutes, stirring occasionally. Stir in refried beans; warm through and remove from heat. In a saucepan over medium-low heat, whisk together salsa, soup and milk; heat through. Spread a layer of salsa mixture in the bottom of a greased 13"x9" baking pan. Divide beef mixture equally among tortillas. Roll up tightly and place in pan, seam-side down. Cover with cheese. Spoon remaining salsa mixture over enchiladas. Bake, uncovered, at 350 degrees for 30 to 45 minutes, until bubbly. Makes 5 servings.

A tasty side for any south-of-the-border main dish...
stir salsa and shredded cheese into hot cooked rice. Cover
and let stand a few minutes, until cheese melts. Olé!

Phony Lasagna

Kathy Reel
Woodway, TX

Three little girls, one of them sick, dad out of town, no lasagna noodles in the cupboard. So I boiled macaroni, layered it in a casserole dish with pasta sauce and cheese on top. Everyone loved it...it has been a family favorite for 20 years now!

16-oz. pkg. elbow macaroni,
   uncooked
32-oz. jar spaghetti sauce
garlic powder and onion powder
   to taste

Optional: 1 lb. ground beef,
   browned and drained
2 c. shredded Cheddar cheese

Cook macaroni according to package directions; drain. In a greased 13"x9" baking pan, mix sauce and seasonings. Gently stir in macaroni and beef, if using. Sprinkle cheese on top. Bake, uncovered, at 350 degrees for 30 minutes, or until hot and bubbly. May be made ahead and refrigerated; bake for one hour. Serves 6.

Ravioli Lasagna

Cindy Ballard
Conway, AR

My daughter and I like spaghetti and lasagna, but my husband and my son don't. My husband likes any kind of ravioli, but I only like the cheese kind. This recipe I touched up to perfection...the whole family loves it and I always have to make two pans!

1 lb. ground beef
1 lb. ground pork sausage
2 28-oz. cans spaghetti sauce,
   divided

2 25-oz. pkgs. frozen cheese
   ravioli, uncooked
3 c. shredded mozzarella cheese,
   divided

Brown beef and sausage in separate skillets over medium heat; drain and set aside. In a greased 13"x9" baking pan, layer half of one can spaghetti sauce, one package frozen ravioli, all of the beef and one cup mozzarella cheese. Repeat layering with remaining sauce, remaining ravioli, all of the sausage and remaining cheese. Cover and bake at 400 degrees for 40 to 45 minutes, until hot and bubbly. Makes 6 to 8 servings.

Dinners for the
Daily Dash

Skillet Chicken Cacciatore

Jennie Gist
Gooseberry Patch

*So delicious! It's really simple to double this recipe,
then freeze half for an easy dinner later on.*

1 onion, cut into wedges
1 green pepper, cut into strips
1 red pepper, cut into strips
1/2 lb. sliced mushrooms
2 T. olive oil
1 lb. boneless, skinless, chicken
 breasts, sliced

26-oz. jar marinara sauce
cooked spaghetti or rice
Garnish: grated Parmesan
 cheese

Heat oil in a large skillet over medium heat. Add vegetables; cook
and stir until tender. Remove vegetables to a bowl. Increase heat to
medium-high. Add chicken; cook until golden and nearly done. Add
pasta sauce and vegetables. Simmer for about 10 minutes, until
chicken is tender, stirring occasionally. Serve over spaghetti or rice,
sprinkled with Parmesan cheese. Serves 4 to 6.

Shells & Cheese Bake

Amy Krumbholz
Bozeman, MT

This casserole was one of my sister's favorites for us kids.

16-oz. pkg. small shell pasta,
 uncooked
1 lb. ground beef or ground
 Italian pork sausage

2 26-oz. jars spaghetti sauce
2 16-oz. pkgs. shredded Italian-
 blend cheese

Cook macaroni according to package directions; drain. Meanwhile,
brown meat in a skillet over medium heat; drain. Combine pasta and
meat in a deep 13"x9" baking pan sprayed with non-stick vegetable
spray. Add sauce; toss to coat. Stir in one package cheese; sprinkle
remaining cheese on top. Bake, uncovered, at 350 degrees for
30 minutes, or until bubbly and cheese melts. Makes 10 servings.

Hamburger-Zucchini One-Dish

Mary Shreve
Dillsburg, PA

My mother started making this easy recipe for me when I was young. I was a very picky eater, especially when it came to vegetables. Now I make it for my kids and they like it too. You can double it and put half in the freezer for another day...just add the cheese topping at serving time.

1/2 lb. ground beef
15-oz. can stewed tomatoes
1/3 c. long-cooking rice, uncooked
2 zucchini, peeled and cut into 1/2-inch cubes

1/2 c. water
2 t. sugar
1 t. onion powder
8-oz. pkg. shredded sharp Cheddar cheese

Brown beef in a large skillet over medium heat; drain. Stir in tomatoes with juice, uncooked rice and remaining ingredients except cheese. Bring to a boil. Reduce heat to medium-low. Cover and simmer for 20 to 25 minutes, stirring occasionally, until rice and zucchini are tender. Top with cheese; let stand until cheese melts. Makes 4 to 6 servings.

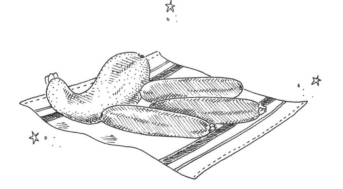

Cool down hot foods before wrapping and freezing. Let just-baked casseroles stand at room temperature for 30 minutes, then chill in the fridge for 30 minutes more. Large pots of soup will cool quickly when set in a sink full of ice water.

Dinners for the
Daily Dash

Hidden Spinach Meatloaf

Nancy Kailihiwa
Wheatland, CA

I started making this meatloaf in an effort to get my kids to eat more vegetables. They used to call the spinach my "special seasoning." Years later, the kids found out what it was, but they still love it for our Sunday supper.

10-3/4 oz. can tomato soup
5 to 10 dashes hot pepper sauce
2 lbs. lean ground beef
1/2 c. onion, finely chopped
10-oz. pkg. frozen chopped
    spinach, thawed and
    well-drained
1/2 c. dry bread crumbs

1/2 c. grated Parmesan cheese
1/2 c. shredded Mozzarella
    cheese
2 eggs, beaten
1 T. Worcestershire sauce
1 t. salt
1/2 t. pepper

In a bowl, combine soup and hot sauce; mix well. Remove 1/2 cup of soup mixture to a large bowl and set the rest aside. Add remaining ingredients to large bowl. Mix well and form into 2 loaves; place in 2 well-greased 9"x5" loaf pans. Bake, uncovered, at 350 degrees for 45 minutes to one hour, until no longer pink in the center. Microwave remaining soup mixture for one minute, or until hot; spread over meatloaves. Second meatloaf may be frozen. Makes 2 meatloaves; each serves 6.

Bake up some mini meatloaves for smaller appetites...
fill muffin tins and bake until done, about 30 minutes.
Pop out mini meatloaves and freeze on a baking sheet,
then pop them out and place in a freezer bag. Later, just
heat up as many as you need.

135

Slow-Simmered Spaghetti Sauce

Maxine Wilson
Kelowna, British Columbia

I don't care much for regular spaghetti sauce, but I love it made in a slow cooker. My kids have always loved this sauce and now they make it for their own kids. Serve hot over your favorite pasta, with garlic bread on the side. Yummy!

1 T. extra-virgin olive oil
2 sweet onions, diced
1 lb. lean ground beef
14-1/2 oz. can stewed tomatoes
15-oz. can tomato sauce
6-oz. can tomato paste
6 stalks celery, thinly sliced

1 t. onion powder
1 t. garlic powder
1 t. dried oregano
1 t. dried thyme
salt and pepper to taste
2 bay leaves

Heat oil in a skillet over medium heat. Add onions; cook until translucent. Add beef; cook until no longer pink. Drain; spoon beef mixture into a slow cooker. Add tomatoes with juice; mash with a potato masher. Stir in remaining ingredients. Cover and cook on low setting for 6 to 8 hours, stirring occasionally. Discard bay leaves before serving. Makes 6 servings.

Turn leftover hot dog buns into slices of garlic bread in a jiffy... easy for little hands to help make. Spread with softened butter, sprinkle with garlic salt and broil until toasty and golden.

Dinners for the
Daily Dash

Meatballs for Spaghetti Sauce *Cherylann Smith*
Hillsborough, NC

*My kids just love homemade spaghetti & meatballs! We have
Spaghetti Night once a week, so I make lots of meatballs all at once.
Then I add two dozen to that night's spaghetti sauce and freeze the
rest in packages of two dozen each.*

3 lbs. ground beef
1 c. Italian-flavored dry
   bread crumbs
1 c. milk
1 egg, beaten
2 T. Italian seasoning

1/4 c. grated Parmesan cheese
1/4 c. dried, minced onion
1 T. salt
1/2 t. pepper
3 cloves garlic, pressed

Combine all ingredients in a large bowl. Mix well and form into
8 dozen small meatballs. Place in ungreased shallow baking pans.
Bake at 350 degrees for 30 minutes, or until meatballs are browned;
drain and cool. Place meatballs on baking sheets; freeze. Divide
meatballs into plastic freezer bags and return to freezer. Makes
8 dozen, about 24 servings.

Make-ahead dishes are perfect for family meals after a
busy day. For an easy side, make a marinated salad to keep
in the fridge...cut up crunchy veggies and toss with
zesty Italian salad dressing.

Enchilada Dippin' Rice

Madonna Alexander
Chicago, IL

A quick and fun Mexican meal! We love watching football games on television. On game nights I try to make something fun to eat. This dish can be made ahead and just heated up later.

1-1/2 to 2 lbs. ground beef
  or turkey
10-oz. can mild red enchilada
  sauce
10-3/4 oz. can Cheddar cheese
  soup
2 c. cooked brown or white rice
16-oz. can refried beans,
  warmed

16-oz. pkg. shredded Mexican-
  blend cheese
Garnish: salsa, sour cream,
  guacamole
Optional: canned sweet corn &
  diced peppers, chopped black
  olives and jalapeño peppers
scoop-type tortilla or corn chips

In a large skillet over medium heat, cook beef or turkey until no longer pink; drain. Add sauce and soup; heat through. Add cooked rice; mix well and remove from heat. Spread beans to cover the bottom of a lightly greased 13"x9" baking pan. Spread meat mixture on top; cover with cheese. Let stand for several minutes, until cheese melts. Garnish as desired; serve with chips for dipping. May also be served as a casserole, with chips crushed and spread on top. Serves 6 to 8.

Food is a wonderful way to learn about other places and cultures! Set the mood with background music...stop by the local library and pick up some CDs of mariachi or salsa music to enjoy at dinnertime.

Dinners for the
Daily Dash

Cream Cheese Chicken & Penne   Rhi Younts
Richmond, IN

I usually make two weeks' worth of freezer meals on Saturdays when my kids are at Grandma's house. This is my favorite recipe...it makes me feel like we're at an Italian restaurant right at home! Serve with a tossed salad and garlic toast.

1/2 c. plus 2 t. butter, sliced
   and divided
0.7-ounce env. Italian salad
   dressing mix
2 lbs. deli roast chicken,
   cut into strips

8-oz. pkg. cream cheese, cubed
10-3/4 oz. can cream of chicken
   soup
1/2 to 1 c. milk
16-oz. pkg. penne pasta,
   uncooked

Melt 1/2 cup butter in a large saucepan over medium heat; stir in salad dressing mix. Add chicken and stir to coat. Add cream cheese; stir until melted. Stir in soup and milk; cook until smooth and creamy. Remove from heat; allow to cool completely. Spoon chicken mixture into a one-gallon plastic freezer bag; double-bag if possible and label with instructions. Lay flat in the freezer. To serve, thaw overnight in the refrigerator. Cook pasta according to package directions. Drain and return to pasta pot; stir in remaining butter to prevent sticking. Add chicken mixture to the same pot; heat through over low heat. Makes 6 to 8 servings.

A full pantry is so reassuring! With pasta, rice, dried beans, favorite sauces, baking mixes and canned soups, veggies and fruit on hand, you're all set to stir up a satisfying meal anytime.

Hawaiian Chicken

Sarah Lundvall
Ephrata, PA

Whenever I want my kids to eat something other than macaroni & cheese, this is my go-to recipe! With a slow cooker, it's easy.

2 lbs. chicken tenders
20-oz. can pineapple chunks
1 green or red pepper, sliced
1/2 c. onion, diced

1/2 c. brown sugar, packed
1/2 c. soy sauce
1-1/2 c. couscous, uncooked

Place chicken in a slow cooker. Add pineapple with juice, pepper, onion, brown sugar and soy sauce. Cover and cook on low setting for 6 to 8 hours. About 30 minutes before serving time, prepare couscous as directed on package. Serve chicken mixture over couscous. Makes 6 servings.

BBQ Chicken in the Crock

Carrie Kelderman
Pella, IA

Instead of turning on my oven in the summertime, I like to make at least two slow-cooker meals each week! This chicken is excellent served as is, or shredded and served over lettuce salads.

3 to 4 lbs. boneless, skinless
    chicken
1 c. catsup

1 T. brown sugar, packed
3 T. Worcestershire sauce

Place chicken into a slow cooker; set aside. Combine remaining ingredients; spoon over chicken. Cover and cook on low setting for 7 to 8 hours. May also be made into a freezer meal. Place chicken in a one-gallon plastic freezer bag; top with sauce ingredients and freeze. To serve, thaw overnight in refrigerator, then prepare in a slow cooker as above. Serves 6.

Safety first! When using a slow cooker, always make sure it's set back far enough on the counter that little hands can't touch it or pull on the cord.

Dinners for the
Daily Dash

Fiesta Chicken & Beans

Rita Jefferis
Anthony, KS

My family loves this slow-cooker dish because it keeps so well all day in the crock to match our busy come & go schedules. Some like it with rice or cornbread and more hot sauce, others enjoy it as a dip with tortilla chips. It's delicious wrapped in a warm flour tortilla too.

2 T. water
6 to 8 chicken thighs
salt and pepper
1/3 c. onion, chopped
2 cloves garlic, chopped
14-1/2 oz. can diced tomatoes
2 15-oz. cans black beans,
    drained and rinsed

1 c. frozen corn
1 c. mild salsa
8-oz. can tomato sauce
1 t. ground cumin
1/2 t. garlic powder
Optional: 1 green or red pepper,
    chopped
cooked rice or cornbread

Add water and chicken to a slow cooker sprayed with non-stick vegetable spray. Season chicken with salt and pepper; top with onion and garlic. In a bowl, mix undrained tomatoes and remaining ingredients except rice or cornbread; spoon over chicken. Cover and cook on low setting for 6 to 8 hours. Remove chicken to a plate; cool slightly and discard skin and bones. Stir chicken back into mixture in slow cooker. Serve ladled over cooked rice or squares of cornbread. Serves 6.

A fast & fun new way to serve cornbread! Mix up the batter, thin slightly with a little extra milk, then bake until crisp in a waffle iron. Top with your favorite Tex-Mex dish, or cut into wedges...terrific for dunking in chili or soup.

Darci's Pizza Burgers

Darci Heaton
Woodbury, PA

Very simple to make and budget-friendly, this slow-cooker recipe can be doubled or tripled for a potluck or party. Make it your own with any spices and extra touches you like. Yummy!

1 lb. ground beef
salt, pepper, onion powder and
   garlic powder to taste
1 to 1-1/2 15-oz. jars
   pizza sauce

1 c. shredded mozzarella cheese
3-oz. pkg. pepperoni, diced
1 t. Italian seasoning
6 to 8 sandwich buns, split
6 to 8 slices mozzarella cheese

Brown beef in a skillet over medium heat; drain. Season with salt, pepper, onion powder and garlic powder. Spoon beef into a slow cooker. Add desired amount of pizza sauce, shredded cheese and pepperoni; stir well. Cover and cook on low setting for 4 hours, or until hot and bubbly. About 30 minutes before serving, sprinkle in Italian seasoning; stir. To serve, spoon onto buns; top with a cheese slice. Makes 6 to 8 servings.

Delicious burgers begin with ground beef chuck labeled as 80/20. A little fat in the beef adds flavor...there's no need to purchase expensive ground sirloin.

Dinners for the
Daily Dash

Alex's Meatball Subs

Krista Marshall
Fort Wayne, IN

After seeing lots of TV commercials for a popular sub shop, my son told me he wanted to try meatball subs. He just knew he would like them and I just had to make them. Well, when Alex asks, Mommy has to try! With a slow cooker, it was a snap.

3 c. frozen Italian meatballs
2 26-oz. jars spaghetti sauce
15-oz. can tomato sauce
14-1/2 oz. can diced tomatoes
1 T. sugar
1 T. Italian seasoning

salt and pepper to taste
8-oz. pkg. shredded mozzarella
    cheese
6 to 8 hoagie buns, split
Garnish: shredded Parmesan
    cheese

Place meatballs in a slow cooker. Add sauces, diced tomatoes with juice, sugar and seasonings. Stir gently to combine. Cover and cook on low setting for 6 to 7 hours. To serve, add some mozzarella cheese to the bottom of each bun; spoon meatballs and sauce over cheese. Add more mozzarella cheese and a sprinkle of Parmesan cheese; close buns. Makes 6 to 8 servings.

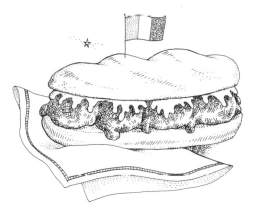

Freeze meatballs individually, then simply pop them into a plastic egg carton. Later you can remove just the number you need...easy!

All-Day Enchiladas

Betty Schaefer
Brazoria, TX

This has been a family favorite for many years. When my kids were in school, I would fill the crock in the morning, then they added the tortillas when they got home. Add a salad and you've got a meal!

1-1/2 lbs. ground beef, browned
   and drained
26-oz. can cream of chicken
   or mushroom soup
10-3/4 oz. can Cheddar
   cheese soup

10-oz. can enchilada sauce
1/2 c. onion, chopped
Optional: 1/4 c. chopped
   green chiles
salt and pepper to taste
12 to 15 corn tortillas, torn

Combine all ingredients except tortillas in a slow cooker; stir. Cover and cook on low setting for 6 to 8 hours. Add tortillas; cover and cook for one additional hour. Makes 8 servings.

Busy Mom's Faux Chili Colorado

Amy Orlovich
Boise, ID

I have three kids in sports activities, so I need slow-cooker recipes that are quick and delicious. All three kids like it...that alone is a miracle! The fact that I can prepare it in five minutes makes it a favorite. Use red or green enchilada sauce as you prefer.

2 to 3-lb. pork roast
19-oz. can enchilada sauce
6 to 8 8-inch flour tortillas

Garnish: shredded cheese,
   sour cream, guacamole,
   diced tomatoes, lettuce

Place roast in a slow cooker; pour enchilada sauce over roast. Cover and cook on low setting for 10 to 12 hours, or on high setting for 4 to 6 hours. To serve, shred pork and place in tortillas with desired toppings. Makes 6 to 8 servings.

Dinners for the
Daily Dash

Sweet & Saucy Meatballs

Lori Roggenbuck
Ubly, MI

*This slow-cooker recipe really saves the day on
busy weeknights! My kids gobble them right down.*

3/4 c. quick-cooking oats,
   uncooked
3 T. onion, finely chopped
1 c. milk
1-1/2 t. salt
1 t. pepper

2 lbs. lean ground beef
1 c. catsup
1/2 c. water
1/4 c. barbecue sauce
2 T. brown sugar, packed
mashed potatoes

In a large bowl, combine oats, onion, milk and seasonings. Crumble
beef over oat mixture; mix well. Form into one-inch balls and place in
a slow cooker. In a separate bowl, combine catsup, water, barbecue
sauce and brown sugar; pour over meatballs. Cover and cook on low
setting for 6 to 8 hours, until meatballs are no longer pink. Serve over
mashed potatoes. Serves 6.

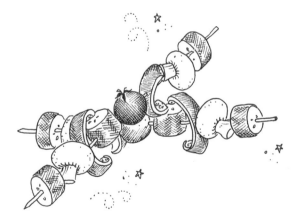

March 28 is National Something-on-a-Stick Day! Kids will
giggle at a meal of meatballs and veggies served on skewers.
For dessert, serve up fruit cubes and marshmallows on sticks,
with hot fudge sauce for dipping. Such fun!

Hearty Beef Stew

Kathleen Kennedy
Renton, WA

*I like to serve this slow-cooker stew with warm biscuits
for an easy meal that kids and guys love.*

2 lbs. stew beef cubes
1/2 c. all-purpose flour
salt and pepper to taste
4 T. oil, divided
4 potatoes, peeled and cubed
6 carrots, peeled and cubed

1-3/4 c. canned diced tomatoes
2 0.87-oz. envs. brown
   gravy mix
10-3/4 oz. can cream of
   mushroom soup
2 c. beef broth or water

Pat beef dry with paper towels; set aside. Combine flour, salt and
pepper in a plastic zipping bag. In small batches, toss beef in bag to
coat. In a heavy skillet, heat 2 tablespoons oil over medium-high heat.
Add beef to skillet in batches, browning on all sides; add a little more
oil as needed. Drain; season beef with additional salt and pepper.
Transfer beef to a slow cooker; add vegetables. In a bowl, whisk
together remaining ingredients. Pour gravy mixture over all; gently stir
to mix. Cover and cook on low setting for 8 to 10 hours. Serves 6.

Be sure to reheat leftovers in the microwave or on the stove.
Reheating in the slow cooker isn't really safe, as it takes too
long for the food to reach the desired internal temperature.

Dinners for the
Daily Dash

Mother's Round Steak Dinner
*LaShelle Brown
Mulvane, KS*

My mother made this slow-cooker dinner often when I was growing up, so we could have a nice home-cooked meal when everyone was home from work and school. It is quick & easy to put together.

1 lb. beef round steak,
    tenderized and cut into
    bite-size pieces
garlic salt and pepper to taste
1/2 onion, sliced and separated
    into rings

2 to 3 potatoes, peeled and
    cubed
14-1/2 oz. can French-style
    green beans, drained
10-3/4 oz. can tomato soup
1/2 c. water

Place beef in a slow cooker; season with garlic salt and pepper. Top with onion, potatoes and beans. Spread with soup; drizzle with water. Cover and cook on low setting for 6 to 8 hours, stirring occasionally. Serves 4 to 6.

All-day slow cooking works wonders on inexpensive, less-tender cuts of beef...arm and chuck roast, rump roast, round steak and stew beef cook up tender and delicious.

Ready When You Are!

Zesty Italian Chicken

Linda Stone
Cookeville, TN

Very easy...just add a few ingredients to your slow cooker and turn it on. Four hours later, a scrumptious dinner is served!

4 boneless, skinless chicken
   breasts
0.7-oz. pkg. zesty Italian salad
   dressing mix
2 10-3/4 oz. cans cream of
   chicken and/or mushroom
   soup

8-oz. pkg. cream cheese,
   softened
Optional: 2 to 3 T. milk
cooked linguine or bowtie pasta

Place chicken in a slow cooker; sprinkle with dressing mix and set aside. In a bowl, blend soup and cream cheese; add milk if a creamier consistency is preferred. Spoon soup mixture over chicken. Cover and cook on low setting for 4 hours, or until chicken is tender. Remove chicken from slow cooker; cool slightly. Shred chicken; return to slow cooker and stir into soup mixture. To serve, spoon over cooked pasta. Serves 4.

A clear plastic over-the-door shoe organizer is super for pantry storage...just slip gravy mix packets, spice jars and other small items into the pockets.

Dinners for the
Daily Dash

Pork Chop Delight

Chelsea Oliver
Arlington, TN

*Love this homestyle recipe! I usually have all the ingredients
on hand and the slow cooker makes it so easy.*

1/2 c. plus 2 T. all-purpose flour,
  divided
salt and pepper to taste
4 to 6 boneless pork chops
2 T. oil

1 onion, sliced
2 c. chicken broth
8-oz. container sour cream
cooked rice or egg noodles

Mix 1/2 cup flour, salt and pepper in a shallow dish; dredge pork
chops. Heat oil in a skillet over medium heat; brown chops on both
sides. In a slow cooker, layer chops with onion slices. Pour broth over
top. Cover and cook on low setting for 7 to 8 hours. Blend sour cream
and remaining flour; stir into cooking juices. Cover and cook on high
setting for 15 to 30 minutes, until thickened. Serve chops and sauce
over cooked rice or noodles. Serves 4 to 6.

Mother's Sausage Supper

Rachel Burch
Illiopolis, IL

*My mom was a nurse and she would toss this in the slow cooker
before leaving for work. When my sister Elizabeth and I got off the
school bus, the house smelled wonderful. Now I'm a homeschooling
mom and this recipe is just as convenient for me. My sister says her
son and his roommates made this dish while at college too.*

6 potatoes, peeled and cubed
3 14-1/2 oz. cans green beans
1 onion, sliced

1 lb. smoked pork sausage,
  cut into 2-inch pieces
salt and pepper to taste

In a slow cooker, layer potatoes, green beans (draining 2 of the cans)
and remaining ingredients. Cover and cook on low setting for 8 hours.
Makes 6 servings.

Brightly colored vintage-style oilcloth makes the best-ever
tablecloth...it wipes clean in a jiffy!

Hot & Zippy Sandwich Loaf

Sue Klapper
Muskego, WI

I love to make this for my family for our Sandwich Night dinner. It comes out all crusty and melty...yummy!

1 loaf unsliced bread,
   about 8 inches long
1/2 c. butter, softened
3 T. onion, minced
3 T. mustard

1 T. poppy seed
1 T. lemon juice
1/8 t. cayenne pepper
12 slices Swiss cheese
12 slices deli salami

Carefully cut top off loaf; make 6 diagonal cuts at equal intervals from top almost through to bottom. Place loaf on a lightly greased baking sheet. In a bowl, mix remaining ingredients except cheese and salami. Set aside 3 tablespoons of butter mixture; spread remaining mixture between cuts in loaf. Alternate 2 cheese slices and 2 salami slices in each cut, allowing slices to partially stick out. Spread reserved butter mixture over top and sides of loaf. Bake, uncovered, at 350 degrees for 25 minutes, until hot and cheese is melted. To serve, slice loaf through between each cut. Makes 6 servings.

From asparagus to zucchini, vegetables come in all shapes and colors! Kids can make fun placemats by clipping colorful pictures of veggies from grocery ads, gardening catalogs and seed packets. Arrange pictures on sheets of construction paper, then top with self-adhesive clear plastic.

Dinners for the
Daily Dash

Heavenly Ham Sammies

Andrea Gordon
Lewis Center, OH

When I was growing up, Mom always had these sandwiches in the freezer for us, only her version was made with diced hot dogs. My family loves honey ham, so that is what I use. They are great to pop in the oven on busy nights.

1-1/2 lbs. thinly sliced deli
   honey ham, diced
10-oz. pkg. shredded Cheddar
   cheese

2 to 3 T. onion, grated
3 T. mayonnaise
3 T. honey mustard
8 hamburger buns, split

In a large bowl, mix together all ingredients except buns. Fill buns with ham mixture, then wrap each sandwich in 2 layers of aluminum foil. Freeze. To serve, place desired number of frozen wrapped sandwiches on a baking sheet. Bake at 350 degrees for 45 minutes, until heated through. Serves 8.

Enjoy a movie night at home...fun for the whole family! Let the kids each invite a special friend and scatter plump cushions on the floor for extra seating. Pass the popcorn, please!

Oven-Fried Chicken

Debbie Mills
Angus, Ontario

A favorite my kids just love! I pop it in the fridge the night before to marinate, then it's quick to bake for dinner.

2 lbs. assorted chicken pieces
1 c. buttermilk
1/4 c. cayenne hot pepper sauce
1/4 c. fresh chives, chopped
3/4 c. all-purpose flour
1/2 c. corn flake cereal

1/2 t. paprika
1/2 t. garlic powder
1/2 t. salt
1/2 t. pepper
2 T. oil

Place chicken in a large glass bowl. Add buttermilk, hot sauce and chives; stir to coat. Cover and refrigerate for 8 to 12 hours. Combine flour, cereal and seasonings in a food processor; pulse until finely crumbled. Pour into a large plastic zipping bag. Remove chicken from marinade; shake off excess. Discard marinade. Add chicken to flour mixture, one piece at a time; shake to coat. Arrange chicken on a greased rimmed baking sheet. Bake, uncovered, at 400 degrees for 30 minutes, or until golden and chicken juices run clear. Serves 4 to 6.

Stir up a frosty pitcher of lemonade. Combine 3 cups water, 1/2 cup sugar and 1/2 cup fresh-squeezed lemon juice. Stir until sugar dissolves and serve over ice...wonderful!

Dinners for the
Daily Dash

Super Chicken Toasted Sandwich

Natalie McKnight
Columbus, OH

This is simple to make, wallet-friendly and tasty!
Serve with chips or pasta salad for a tasty casual meal.

2 T. Caesar salad dressing
1 to 2 t. butter, softened
1 loaf Italian bread, halved
   lengthwise

2 c. deli roast chicken, shredded
1-1/2 c. shredded Swiss cheese
Garnish: lettuce, salad dressing,
   other sandwich toppings

Mix salad dressing and butter. Spread on cut sides of loaf; place on a baking sheet. Bake at 400 degrees for 5 to 7 minutes, until lightly toasted. Remove from oven. Place chicken on half of loaf; top with cheese. Return to oven until cheese is melted, about 5 minutes. Top with lettuce, more salad dressing if desired and any other toppings. Cut and serve. Makes 4 servings.

Kid-Friendly Grilled Chicken

Jenny Bishoff
Mountain Lake Park, MD

Too many grilled chicken recipes leave the chicken dry or are just
too complicated for lazy summer days...but my kids love this one!

1/2 c. Italian salad dressing
1 T. honey

1 t. lime juice
1 lb. chicken tenders

Mix salad dressing, honey and lime juice in a bowl. Add chicken; cover and refrigerate for 3 to 8 hours. Drain, discarding marinade. Grill chicken over medium heat for 3 to 4 minutes per side, until golden and juices run clear. Makes 4 servings.

Take time everyday to do something silly.
– Philippa Walker

So-Easy Chicken Alfredo

Wendy Jo Minotte
Duluth, MN

This is the recipe I always turn to when we're short on time and need a speedy supper with wonderful flavor. It never fails to please!

16-oz. pkg. fettuccine pasta,
  uncooked
1/2 c. butter, sliced
8-oz. pkg. cream cheese, cubed
1 c. milk
1/3 c. grated Parmesan cheese

13-oz. can chicken breast,
  drained and flaked
salt and pepper to taste
Garnish: grated Parmesan
  cheese

Cook pasta according to package directions; drain. Meanwhile, melt butter in a saucepan over medium heat. When butter is almost melted, add cream cheese; mix well. Add milk, Parmesan cheese and chicken. Stir with a whisk until well blended. Add salt and pepper to taste. Serve over pasta, sprinkled with additional grated cheese. Makes 6 servings.

Make a game of table talk! Write fun questions on file cards. What kind of animal would you like to be? If you had three wishes, what would you ask for? Where in the world would you like to travel to? and so on. Each night, you can pull a different card to talk about with the kids.

Dinners for the
Daily Dash

Spicy Italian Chicken

Jody Keiper
Crystal Lake, IL

These chicken breasts are tender and juicy...this is my daughter's favorite! She asks for this meal frequently, and I don't mind because it is so easy and healthy.

4 boneless, skinless chicken
   breasts
Italian seasoning to taste

1/8 t. salt
1 t. cracked pepper
2 T. olive oil

Coat chicken on both sides with Italian seasoning; sprinkle with salt and pepper. Heat olive oil in a skillet over medium heat. Add chicken; cook until golden on both sides. Cover and cook for 5 minutes. Uncover and cook 5 minutes more, or until chicken juices run clear. Makes 4 servings.

Make a simple, kid-friendly side that's ready to serve in a jiffy with a package of angel hair pasta. Toss cooked pasta with a little butter and grated Parmesan cheese, or try chopped tomato and a drizzle of olive oil.

Quick Beef & Bean Tacos

Carolyn Deckard
Bedford, IN

This is a great after-school snack or an early dinner for my grandkids before they go off to one of their sport events. It's a quick way of fixing something they all like...that doesn't happen often!

1 lb. ground beef
1/4 c. onion, chopped
15-oz. can chili with beans
1/4 c. water

10 corn taco shells
Garnish: shredded Cheddar
   cheese, sour cream, shredded
   lettuce, diced tomato

In a skillet over medium heat, brown beef with onion. Drain; stir in soup and water. Reduce heat to low; cover and simmer for 5 to 10 minutes. Divide beef mixture among taco shells. Add toppings as desired. Makes 10 servings.

Take advantage of grocery specials on ground beef for easy, economical family meals! Crumble several pounds of beef into a baking pan and bake at 350 degrees until browned through, stirring often. Drain well and pack recipe-size portions in freezer bags.

Dinners for the
Daily Dash

Farmhouse BBQ Muffin Cups

*Tina George
El Dorado, AR*

*While stationed in Okinawa, my fellow home-school moms and
I enjoyed trading simple but delicious recipes to serve our busy
families. This one came from my friend Leslie. These BBQ muffin cups
were always quick and easy to get on the table. Serve with buttered
corn on the cob and you've got a meal!*

1 lb. ground beef
1/2 c. onion, chopped
1 c. barbecue sauce

16.3-oz. can jumbo buttermilk
   biscuits
1 c. shredded Cheddar cheese

In a skillet over medium heat, brown beef and onion. Drain; stir in
barbecue sauce. Pat each biscuit into a 4 to 5-inch circle; press each
biscuit into an ungreased muffin cup. Spoon beef mixture into biscuit
cups; sprinkle with cheese. Bake at 375 degrees for about 15 minutes,
until biscuits are golden and cheese is melted. Makes 6 to 8 servings.

My theory on housework is, if the item doesn't multiply,
smell, catch on fire, or block the refrigerator door, let it be.
No one cares. Why should you?

–Erma Bombeck

Bacon Cheeseburger Sloppy Joes

Rachel Kowasic
Valrico, FL

My family loves to eat Sloppy Joes! I still remember when my mom used to make them for us with canned sauce. This is my updated take on the recipe...it's a hit with everyone!

6 slices bacon
1 lb. ground turkey
1/3 c. mayonnaise
1/4 c. catsup
1 T. pickle relish

1 T. mustard
2 t. Worcestershire sauce
6 hamburger buns, split
6 slices Monterey Jack cheese
6 T. French fried onions

In a skillet over medium heat, cook bacon until crisp; set bacon aside on a paper towel. Partially drain drippings in skillet. Add turkey; cook until browned. Stir in mayonnaise, catsup, relish, mustard and Worcestershire sauce; heat through. To serve, top each bun with one cheese slice, one tablespoon onions, one slice bacon and some of the turkey mixture. Serves 6.

A mini photo album is just right for keeping tried & true recipes handy on the kitchen counter. Slide in a few snapshots of happy family mealtimes too!

Dinners for the
Daily Dash

Italian Breaded Steak

Cheri Koshiol
Maplewood, MN

My mom made this dish once a month, and I have carried on the tradition. My kids are excited all day for dinner! I usually serve this with mashed potatoes or pasta and a veggie.

2 to 4 lbs. beef round steak, thinly sliced	1 c. vegetable oil
	3 T. olive oil
2 eggs, beaten	
1 c. Italian-flavored dry bread crumbs	

Dip beef into eggs, then into bread crumbs. Chill for about one hour. Heat oils in a large skillet over medium-high heat. Add beef to skillet; cook until golden on both sides. Serves 6 to 8.

Kid-Friendly Meatloaf

Shonnie Sims
Canton, GA

My kids really enjoy this meatloaf. It has no onions or peppers but is still full of flavor. It's a real kid-pleaser!

1 to 2 lbs. ground beef	1/4 c. mustard
2 eggs, beaten	1/2 to 3/4 c. catsup
1 sleeve saltine crackers, crushed	Optional: additional catsup

In a large bowl, combine all ingredients except optional catsup. Mix well and form into a loaf; place in a greased 13"x9" baking pan. Top with more catsup, if desired. Bake, uncovered, at 350 degrees for 40 to 45 minutes, until no longer pink in the center. Serves 6 to 8.

Keep a permanent marker handy in the kitchen to write the purchase date on food cans and packages...you'll always know which ones to use first.

Taco Ravioli Bake

Sherri Hamar
West Mifflin, PA

My kids love ravioli! We have it at least once a week. My son asked if I could do something a little different, so I tried adding some taco mix. It was the biggest hit ever! Now any time they have friends over, this is what my kids ask me to make.

1-1/2 lbs. ground beef
1-1/4 oz. pkg. taco seasoning
   mix
3/4 c. water
40-oz. pkg. frozen beef ravioli
   with sauce

8-oz. pkg. shredded Cheddar
   cheese
Optional: sliced black olives,
   chopped onion

Brown beef in a skillet over medium heat; drain. Stir in seasoning mix and water; simmer for 8 to 10 minutes. Place ravioli in a lightly greased 13"x9" baking pan. Spoon beef mixture over ravioli; top with cheese. Bake, uncovered, at 350 degrees for 25 to 30 minutes, until bubbly and cheese is melted. Garnish with olives and onion. Makes 6 servings.

Feeding a crowd? Serve festive Mexican, Italian or Chinese-style dishes that everybody loves. They usually feature rice or pasta, so they're filling yet budget-friendly. The theme makes it a snap to put together the menu and table decorations too.

Dinners for the
Daily Dash

Cowgirl Up & Cornbread

Jennifer Rubino
Hickory, NC

What do you do when everyone's hungry and you're out of time?
Cowgirl up! This tasty chow is ready in less than 30 minutes.

8-1/2 oz. pkg. corn muffin mix
1 to 1-1/2 lbs. lean ground beef
1/2 onion, diced

22-oz. can smoky baked beans
11-oz. can corn, drained

Prepare and bake cornbread according to package directions.
Meanwhile, brown beef and onion in a skillet over medium heat; drain.
Add beans and corn to beef mixture; heat through. Serve beef mixture
over squares of warm cornbread. Serves 4.

A large unfolded map makes a very clever table topper!
Sure to spark conversations about places you've been
and spots you'd like to visit.

Chuck Wagon Mac

Vicki Lanzendorf
Madison, WI

*One of my favorites when I was a kid, and it still is to this day.
Any leftovers are tasty too...although with a 17-year-old son
who's well over 6 feet tall, leftovers are rare!*

7-1/4 oz. pkg. macaroni &
  cheese mix
1 lb. ground beef
1/2 c. celery, sliced

1/2 c. onion, diced
2 c. frozen corn, thawed
6-oz. can tomato paste
salt and pepper to taste

Prepare macaroni & cheese mix as package directs. Meanwhile, brown
beef in a skillet over medium heat; drain. Add celery and onion to beef;
cook until tender. Stir in corn, tomato paste, salt and pepper; mix with
prepared macaroni & cheese. Spoon into a greased 2-quart casserole
dish. Bake, uncovered, at 350 degrees for 20 minutes, or until heated
through. Makes 6 servings.

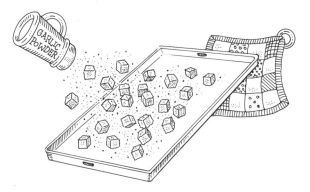

Turn leftover slices of bread into tasty salad croutons. Cut
bread into cubes and toss with olive oil, garlic powder and
dried herbs. Bake on a baking sheet at 400 degrees for 5 to
10 minutes, until toasty and golden.

Dinners for the
Daily Dash

Hamburger Roll-Ups

Angela Shurtleff
Haines, OR

I received this recipe from an old family friend when I was first married, over twenty years ago. It's very easy, cheap and filling. My kids are always asking me to make it.

1 lb. ground beef
1/4 c. onion, diced
salt and pepper to taste
1 loaf frozen bread dough,
    thawed

1 c. shredded Cheddar cheese
3 T. butter, melted
Optional: catsup

Brown beef with onion, salt and pepper in a skillet over medium heat; drain. Meanwhile, on a floured surface, roll out dough into a 15-inch by 12-inch rectangle. Spoon beef mixture over dough; sprinkle with cheese. Roll up, starting on one long edge. Cut into rolls, about 1-1/2 inches wide. Place rolls cut-side down on a greased baking sheet; brush with melted butter. Cover with plastic wrap sprayed with non-stick vegetable spray; let rise for 30 minutes. Uncover; bake at 350 degrees for 25 to 30 minutes, until golden. Serve with catsup for dipping, if desired. Serves 6 to 8.

Grow a windowsill garden...fun for kids to try! Fill a jar with water, then use toothpicks to suspend a fresh carrot top in the water. Place the jar in a sunny window...the new plant will form roots and leaves in just a few days.

Mimi's Spaghetti & Chicken

Janice Fry
Hoover, AL

My mother gave me this versatile recipe when my five children were small, saying I would have most of the ingredients in my pantry. As a busy mom, I used this recipe almost every week because it was easy, the kids loved it and, most of all, it was cheap! Now, my children are grown and married with children and guess what? This recipe continues on in each of their kitchens! It's a life-saver!

8-oz. pkg. angel hair pasta, uncooked
12-1/2 oz. can chicken, drained and flaked
10-3/4 oz. can cream of chicken or celery soup
1 c. sour cream
1/2 c. onion, grated
1 t. garlic salt
1/8 t. Cajun seasoning or paprika
salt and pepper to taste
Optional: green peppers or green chiles, diced
1 to 2 c. shredded Cheddar cheese
1 to 2 2.8-oz. cans French fried onions

Cook pasta according to package directions, just until tender; drain. Meanwhile, mix together remaining ingredients except cheese and French fried onions; set aside. Transfer pasta to a greased 13"x9" baking pan; add chicken mixture and stir gently. Top with cheese. Bake, uncovered, at 350 degrees for 20 to 30 minutes, until bubbly and cheese has melted. Top with onions during the last 5 to 7 minutes of baking time. Serves 6.

No peeking when there's a casserole in the oven!
Every time the oven door is opened, the temperature drops
at least 25 degrees...dinner will take longer to bake.

Dinners for the
Daily Dash

Dirty Rice

Leea Mercer
League City, TX

My kids just love this recipe! The name makes them giggle too. If you like, replace the cream of onion soup with a second can of cream of mushroom, and brown some chopped onion with the beef.

1 lb. ground beef
2 to 3 cloves garlic, chopped
salt and pepper to taste
2 c. instant rice, uncooked
1 to 2 cubes chicken bouillon

10-3/4 oz. can cream of
   mushroom soup
10-3/4 oz. can cream of onion
   soup

Brown beef in a skillet over medium heat, adding garlic when beef is nearly done. Drain; season with salt and pepper. Meanwhile, in a separate saucepan, cook rice according to package directions, adding bouillon to rice as it cooks. Add cooked rice and soups to the browned beef. Stir in a little water to the desired consistency. Simmer until heated through, about 10 minutes. Serves 4.

Oversized clear glass jars make attractive canisters for storing macaroni, dried beans and rice...no more messy half-used packages in the pantry. Because the contents are visible, you'll always know when it's time to restock.

Cheeseburger Cauliflower

Renae Scheiderer
Beallsville, OH

Low-carb and tasty! My daughter Emily always eats her veggies when I make this simple dish.

1-1/2 lbs. ground beef
1 lb. fresh or frozen cauliflower
   flowerets
1/2 t. garlic salt
salt to taste
1 c. shredded Cheddar cheese

Brown beef in a skillet over medium heat; drain. Meanwhile, in a separate saucepan, cover cauliflower with water. Cook over medium heat until tender, about 15 minutes. If using frozen cauliflower, prepare according to package directions. Drain cauliflower well; add to beef along with seasonings and cheese. Cook until heated through and cheese is melted. Serves 4 to 6.

A dinner of leftovers is more fun when you call it Family Buffet Night. Set out individual servings of casseroles in pretty dishes, toss veggies into a salad and add a basket of warm rolls. Arrange everything on a counter...everyone is sure to come looking for his or her favorites!

Dinners for the *Daily Dash*

Gam's Stuffed Zucchini

Lisa Engwell
Bellevue, NE

When I was growing up, my parents struggled many times to make ends meet on an enlisted military budget. They grew a huge garden to help with the cost of food. Mom (Gam to her grandchildren) came up with this recipe as an economical dinner to feed our family. It's very filling and very comforting. It's great meatless as well. One of our favorites from the garden!

6.9-oz. pkg. chicken-flavored
   rice vermicelli mix
Optional: 6-oz. can tuna,
   drained and flaked
4 medium zucchini, trimmed

salt to taste
1/2 c. shredded Muenster,
   mozzarella or Monterey
   Jack cheese
1 tomato, chopped

Prepare rice vermicelli mix as label directs. When done, stir in tuna, if using. Meanwhile, place whole zucchini in a large saucepan; cover with water. Cook over medium-high heat until crisp-tender; drain and let cool. Cut zucchini in half lengthwise. Using tip of spoon, scoop out zucchini halves, leaving shells about 1/4 to 1/2-inch thick. Arrange zucchini halves cut-side up in a greased 13"x9" baking pan; sprinkle lightly with salt. Spoon some of the rice mixture into each zucchini half; top with cheese and tomato. Bake, uncovered, at 375 degrees for 10 minutes, or until rice is heated through and cheese melts. Makes 8 servings.

Start family meals with a gratitude circle...each person takes a moment to share two or three things that he or she is thankful for that day. It's a sure way to put everyone in a cheerful mood!

Donnita's Saucy Dogs

Wendy Ball
Battle Creek, MI

This is a recipe created by my mother-in-law, who passed away in 2011. She was pretty savvy in stretching the dollar for a family of ten. Though she hardly ever wrote down any recipes, my husband and I remember how good they tasted. So we worked at getting this recipe just right to remember her by.

3 T. oil
1 lb. hot dogs, quartered
   and diced
1/4 c. all-purpose flour
1/2 c. catsup
1/2 c. water
1/2 t. dry mustard
1/2 t. Worcestershire sauce
3/4 t. kosher salt
1/8 t. pepper
12 hot dog buns, split
1 c. shredded Cheddar cheese
Garnish: catsup, mustard

Heat oil in a skillet over medium heat. Add hot dogs and cook until crisp and golden; drain. Sprinkle hot dogs with flour to coat. Add remaining ingredients except buns, cheese and garnish; heat through. Top buns with equal amounts of hot dog mixture; sprinkle with cheese. Wrap buns individually in aluminum foil; place on a baking sheet. Bake at 350 degrees for 10 to 15 minutes, until cheese is melted. Serve with additional condiments, as desired. Serves 6 to 8.

Take time to share family stories and traditions with your kids. A cherished family recipe can be a great conversation starter at dinner.

Dinners for the
Daily Dash

Country Picnic Drumsticks

*Hannah Hopkins
Plainfield, VT*

*Not only for picnics...these flavorful drumsticks are
awesome for any meal, indoors or out!*

1/3 c. butter, sliced	2 T. onion soup mix
1/3 c. saltine crackers, crushed	8 chicken drumsticks

Make Cucumber Dip ahead of time; chill. Heat oven to 350 degrees.
Place butter in a 13"x9" baking pan; melt butter in oven. In a shallow
dish, stir together crushed crackers and soup mix. Dip drumsticks into
melted butter; coat with crumb mixture. Arrange drumsticks in the
pan; sprinkle with any remaining crumb mixture. Bake, uncovered, at
350 degrees for 45 to 55 minutes, until golden and fork-tender. Serve
chicken hot or cold with Cucumber Dip. Serves 4 to 6.

Cucumber Dip:

1 c. cucumber, peeled and diced	1/2 t. dill weed
8-oz. container sour cream	1/2 t. salt
1-1/2 t. fresh chives, chopped	

Combine all ingredients; mix well. Cover and chill for one hour.

Be ready for spur-of-the-moment picnics with the kids...
tuck a basket filled with picnic supplies into the
car trunk along with a quilt to sit on.

Frugal BBQ Surprise Buns

Cathy Moore
Visalia, CA

People are always surprised to find out what this recipe is made with!
My husband is not usually a tuna fan, yet he was on his second
helping before I told him. It's now one of his favorites.

1 white onion, finely chopped
1 green pepper, finely chopped
1 T. oil
18-oz. bottle bold and spicy
   barbecue sauce

4 6-oz. cans tuna in water,
   well-drained
6 to 10 hamburger buns, split

In a skillet over medium heat, sauté onion and green pepper in oil until
onion is slightly caramelized; drain. Add desired amount of barbecue
sauce; heat through. Add tuna and shred well; heat through. To serve,
spoon onto buns. Makes 6 to 10 servings.

Salmon Patties

Vicki Chambliss
Louisville, MS

This recipe is the only way I can get my kids to eat salmon!

15-oz. can salmon, well-drained
2 eggs, beaten
3/4 to 1 sleeve round buttery
   crackers, crushed

red pepper flakes, dried parsley,
   salt and pepper to taste

Place salmon in a bowl. Discard skin and bones; mash with a fork. Stir
in eggs. Add crushed crackers until mixture is stiff, but not too dry.
Add seasonings. Form into 6 patties. Place in a skillet sprayed with
non-stick vegetable spray. Cook over medium heat until patties are
golden on both sides. Serves 6.

It's easy to freshen up yesterday's crusty rolls or loaf
of bread. Simply sprinkle with water and bake at
400 degrees for 6 to 8 minutes.

KIDS IN THE
Kitchen

Macaroni Pizza Pie

Bianca Erickson
Hidden Valley Lake, CA

My mom, her friend Inge and I came up with this recipe when I was little. It was always a special dinner to make as we didn't make it very often, usually on cold winter nights in between Thanksgiving and Christmas. It's fun for the kids to make and it's so delicious!

7-1/4 oz. pkg. macaroni & cheese mix
2 eggs, beaten
8-oz. can tomato sauce
4-oz. can sliced mushrooms, drained
1/4 c. sliced black olives, drained

1/4 c. green pepper, chopped
1/4 c. onion, chopped
1 t. dried oregano
1 t. dried basil
1 c. pepperoni slices
1 c. shredded mozzarella cheese

Prepare macaroni & cheese according to package directions. Add eggs; mix well. Spread in a well-greased 2-quart casserole dish. Bake, uncovered, at 375 degrees for 10 minutes; remove from oven. In a bowl, stir together tomato sauce, vegetables and herbs. Spoon sauce mixture over baked macaroni & cheese. Arrange pepperoni slices on top; sprinkle with cheese. Bake, uncovered, for 10 more minutes, until bubbly and cheese is melted. Serves 3 to 4.

Kids love to cook, so let them take turns selecting and helping prepare dinner at least once a week. Even if they choose PB&J sandwiches or boxed mac & cheese, they'll be learning basic kitchen skills.

Kids in the *Kitchen*

Tomato-Beef Cavatappi Casserole

Sharon Gutierrez
Litchfield Park, AZ

This dish was a favorite of my two sons Ernie and Dave when they were growing up. They're now in their 30s and they still always request it when they visit. It's simple to toss together...add a crisp salad and warm bread for an easy dinner. It's great to take to a potluck too.

16-oz. pkg. cavatappi pasta or
    elbow macaroni, uncooked
1 lb. ground beef chuck
1/2 t. onion salt or onion powder

1/2 t. garlic salt or garlic powder
Optional: salt and pepper to taste
2 8-oz. cans tomato sauce
2 c. shredded Cheddar cheese

Cook pasta according to package directions; drain. Add pasta to a 13"x9" baking pan sprayed with non-stick vegetable spray; set aside. Brown beef in a skillet over medium heat; drain and add seasonings as desired. Stir in tomato sauce. Reduce heat to low; simmer for 10 minutes. Spoon beef mixture over pasta; stir gently to coat with sauce. Sprinkle with cheese. Cover with aluminum foil. Bake at 350 degrees for 15 to 30 minutes, until hot and bubbly. Let stand 10 minutes before serving. Makes 8 servings.

Before beginning any recipe, wash up! To ensure kids wash thoroughly, encourage them to sing "Row, Row, Row Your Boat" while using lots of soap and warm water. Then dry well.

Dragon Fingers & Dipping Sauce

Pam Halter
Pennsville, NJ

When my daughter Mary was diagnosed with hypoglycemia at age seven, I worked to come up with low-carb meals she would like. This recipe uses very little flour, while the dip has honey and just a touch of sugar in the catsup. We thought it was more fun to call it Dragon Fingers instead of simply "chicken strips." She's grown now, but this remains one of her favorite meals.

1 lb. boneless, skinless chicken breasts, cut into thin strips	1 t. garlic salt
3/4 c. half-and-half	1/2 to 1 t. chili powder
1 c. all-purpose flour	1 t. dried basil
1/4 c. grated Parmesan cheese	pepper to taste
	oil for frying

Make Honey-Mustard Dipping Sauce ahead of time; refrigerate. Cover chicken with half-and-half in a bowl; let stand for 30 minutes. In a separate bowl, combine flour, cheese and seasonings. Add 1/4 inch of oil to a skillet over medium-high heat. When oil is hot, dredge chicken in flour mixture; add carefully to oil. Cook until golden and juices no longer run pink, adding more oil if needed. Drain chicken on a paper towel-lined plate. Serve with Dipping Sauce. Serves 4.

Honey-Mustard Dipping Sauce:

1/2 c. mayonnaise	2 t. catsup
2 T. honey	1 t. garlic, minced
2 T. Dijon mustard	

Mix all ingredients; cover and refrigerate at least 2 hours. Tastes best when made the day before.

A serrated plastic knife is perfect for beginning cooks.
They'll be able to practice cutting ingredients safely,
with all fingers kept above the blade.

Kids in the *Kitchen*

Grammy's Potato Wedges

Sara Tatham
Plymouth, NH

My grandkids love it when these potato wedges are on the menu.
They go very well with hot dogs, hamburgers, meat loaf,
grilled chicken...really, almost any meal!

4 baking potatoes
3 T. olive oil
3 T. grated Parmesan or Romano
   cheese

1 t. paprika
1 t. salt
1/2 t. pepper
garlic powder to taste

Scrub potatoes; do not peel. Cut each potato lengthwise into 8 wedges. Add to a gallon-size plastic zipping bag; drizzle with oil. Seal bag well; shake until potato wedges are coated with oil. Combine remaining ingredients in a cup; mix well and sprinkle over potato wedges. Seal bag again; shake until potato wedges are coated with seasoning mixture. Line a baking sheet with aluminum foil; spray with non-stick vegetable spray. Arrange potato wedges in a single layer on baking sheet. Bake, uncovered, at 350 degrees for one hour, or until tender and golden. Serves 4 to 6.

Show little ones how to measure dry ingredients like flour.
Fill the measuring cup with the ingredient, heaping it up
just a bit over the top. Now take a spatula and level it off.
Measuring spoons work the same way.

Impossible Taco Pie

Dawn Romero
Lewisville, TX

*My mother used to make this beefy pie for dinner
when I was growing up. I loved it...I still do!*

1 lb. ground beef
1/2 c. onion, chopped
4-oz. can chopped green chiles,
   drained
1-1/4 oz. pkg. taco seasoning
   mix
1-1/4 c. milk

3 eggs
3/4 c. biscuit baking mix
1 c. shredded Monterey Jack or
   Cheddar cheese
Garnish: shredded lettuce, diced
   tomatoes, sour cream

In a skillet over medium heat, cook beef and onion until beef is brown;
drain. Stir in chiles and taco seasoning mix. Spoon beef mixture into a
greased 10" deep-dish quiche pan or pie plate; set aside. In a bowl,
beat milk, eggs and baking mix until smooth; pour batter over beef
mixture. Bake at 400 degrees for 25 minutes, or until a knife tip
inserted in center and edges comes out clean. Sprinkle with cheese;
bake for 8 to 10 minutes longer. Let stand 5 minutes before cutting
into wedges. Garnish with lettuce, tomatoes and sour cream, as
desired. Makes 6 servings.

Children are sure to be helpful in the kitchen when they're
wearing their very own kid-size aprons. Select fabric crayons
and plain canvas aprons at a craft store, then let kids decorate
their apron as they like. Follow package directions to
make the design permanent.

Kids in the *Kitchen*

Cheeseburger Cups

Katie Majeske
Denver, PA

When my children were little, this was always a good stand-by
for supper. They liked to help by putting the biscuits in the pan.
Slices of American cheese may be used, if preferred.

1 lb. ground beef
1/2 c. catsup
2 T. brown sugar, packed
1 T. mustard

1-1/2 t. Worcestershire sauce
12-oz. tube refrigerated biscuits
1 c. shredded Cheddar cheese

Brown beef in a skillet over medium heat; drain. Stir in catsup, brown
sugar, mustard and Worcestershire sauce; heat through. Press each
biscuit into the bottom and up the sides of a greased muffin cup. Spoon
beef mixture into cups; top with cheese. Bake at 400 degrees for
15 minutes, or until bubbly and golden. Serves 5.

Baked Sweet Potato Fries

Jill Ball
Highland, UT

A healthier version of French fries that's really tasty.
My family loves them and they are so easy to make.

1 T. olive oil
1/2 t. paprika
8 sweet potatoes, peeled and
   sliced into wedges

Optional: cinnamon, sugar

In a large bowl, mix oil and paprika. Add potato wedges; stir to coat.
Place potato wedges in a single layer on a lightly greased baking sheet.
Bake, uncovered, at 40 degrees for 40 minutes, or until tender and
golden. If desired, sprinkle lightly with cinnamon and sugar. Serves 8.

Teach kids to be careful around a hot stove...roll up
your sleeves, use a thick, dry oven mitt or potholder
and always ask Mom for permission first!

Momma's Mini Meatloaf

Kim Papadopoulos
Largo, FL

I have made this recipe since my oldest child was little. She would help me with all the mixing...it was a fun experience for us both.

1 lb. ground beef, turkey or
   chicken
1 egg, beaten
1/3 c. brown sugar, packed
2 T. honey mustard

3 T. catsup
2 cloves garlic, minced
1 c. dry bread crumbs or
   crackers, crushed
salt and pepper to taste

Combine all ingredients in a large bowl; mix well. Form into 2 separate loaves and place on a greased baking sheet. May also divide into 4 mini loaf pans. Bake at 350 degrees for 35 minutes, or until no longer pink in the center. To serve, cut each loaf in half. Makes 4 servings.

Super-Easy Scalloped Potatoes

Judy Henfey
Cibolo, TX

A very easy kid-friendly recipe to get your children interested in cooking! When my son was much younger, we tried adding chopped ham, fresh peas and even more cheese. We like to sprinkle Parmesan cheese over the top during the last few minutes of cooking.

10-3/4 oz. can cream of
   mushroom soup
3/4 c. milk
4 potatoes, peeled and sliced
   1/8-inch thick

1/2 c. onion, chopped
salt, pepper and dried parsley
   to taste
1 c. shredded Cheddar cheese

Spray a microwave-safe 2-quart casserole dish lightly with non-stick vegetable spray. Add soup and milk; whisk together. Gently stir in remaining ingredients. Cover and microwave on high setting for 10 minutes; stir. Microwave another 12 minutes, or until potatoes are tender. Serves 8.

Kids in the *Kitchen*

Microwave Mac & Cheese

Brenda Saylor
Franklin, OH

I began making this recipe when my children were very young and it instantly became a family favorite. It's so easy, I am always being asked for the recipe. Now they make it for their own families. My daughter-in-law sometimes adds browned ground beef to make it a real one-dish dinner.

2 c. elbow macaroni, uncooked
2 T. butter
2 T. all-purpose flour
1/2 t. salt
1/4 t. pepper

1-3/4 c. milk
1-1/2 to 2 c. shredded Cheddar
  cheese
1/4 c. dry bread crumbs
1/2 t. paprika

Cook macaroni according to package directions; drain. Meanwhile, place butter in a microwave-safe 13"x9" baking pan. Microwave on high setting for 20 to 30 seconds, or until butter is melted. Stir in flour, salt and pepper; gradually stir in milk. Microwave on high setting for about 8 minutes, stirring occasionally, until thickened. Add cheese; stir until melted. Add cooked macaroni; stir gently until coated. Mix bread crumbs and paprika; sprinkle over top. Microwave an additional 2 to 3 minutes, until bubbly. Serves 6.

Microwave recipes are great for little ones learning to cook, since the microwave itself doesn't get hot. Be sure to teach them, though, that the cooked dish will be very hot, as will the steam from a covered dish.

Super-Easy Pizza Dough

Jen Licon-Connor
Gooseberry Patch

With this tried & true recipe, homemade pizza is even easy enough for a weeknight! My daughters and I make this pizza dough all the time.

1 c. warm water
1 t. olive oil
1 t. sugar
1 env. active dry yeast
3-1/2 c. all-purpose
  flour

garlic powder, dried oregano,
  dried basil, salt and/or
  pepper to taste
Garnish: pizza sauce, shredded
  mozzarella cheese, favorite
  pizza toppings

Heat water until very warm, about 110 to 115 degrees; pour into a large bowl. Add olive oil, sugar and yeast; stir to dissolve and set aside. In a separate bowl, combine flour and seasonings, as desired. Add 2 cups flour mixture to yeast mixture, one cup at a time; stir until dough is easy to handle. Knead dough on a floured surface until no longer sticky, adding remaining flour mixture as needed. Cover with a tea towel; let rise for 30 minutes. Flatten dough to desired thickness on a round pizza pan. Bake at 400 degrees for 10 to 12 minutes; let cool for several minutes. Spread with sauce; add cheese and toppings as desired. Bake at 400 degrees for an additional 15 minutes, until crust is golden and cheese is melted. Cut into wedges to serve. Makes 8 servings.

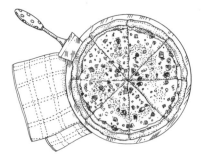

A make-it-yourself pizza party is great for pizza-loving youngsters! It's cheaper than ordering from a pizza shop and doubles as a fun party activity. Set out ready-to-bake pizza crusts and lots of toppings and let party guests be creative!

Kids in the *Kitchen*

Pizza Sammies

Tina Butler
Royse City, TX

These little pizzas are perfect for small hands! Everyone can make their very own personal pizza just the way they like it.

12 frozen dinner rolls, thawed
12-oz. jar pizza sauce
2 to 3 c. shredded mozzarella
   cheese

Garnish: favorite pizza
   toppings

Preheat oven to 200 degrees. Spray baking sheets with non-stick vegetable spray. Place thawed rolls on baking sheets, at least 3 inches apart. Once oven is hot, turn it off. Place baking sheets in oven and leave for exactly 30 minutes; remove from oven. With your hands, flatten rolls into 4-inch circles. Top each circle with one to 2 tablespoons sauce; add cheese and desired toppings. Bake at 350 degrees for 12 to 18 minutes, until cheese is melted and crusts are golden on the bottom. Makes 12 servings.

Crisp Zucchini Sticks

Diane Fliss
Arvada, CO

My mom gave me this recipe that's a healthy alternative to French fries. Even zucchini-hating kids will love these!

1/2 c. egg substitute
1/3 c. Italian-seasoned dry bread
   crumbs

1/4 c. grated Parmesan cheese
3 to 4 zucchini, cut into thick
   sticks about 3" long

Place egg substitute in a shallow bowl; combine bread crumbs and cheese in a separate bowl. Dip zucchini sticks into egg substitute, covering well; coat with crumb mixture. Arrange in a single layer on a baking sheet sprayed with butter-flavored baking spray. Spray tops generously with butter spray. Bake at 450 degrees for 20 to 25 minutes, until crisp and golden. Serve immediately. Serves 4.

Mommy's Hibachi Chicken & Rice

Vivian Tapanes
Fort Myers, FL

My son Richie came up with the idea and name for this recipe because he loves going to the Japanese hibachi restaurant where they cook in front of you. I tried to copy how they made their chicken & rice...and voilà! My family says it tastes even better than the restaurant's. Now it's a family favorite.

12-oz. pkg. steamable frozen
    Asian mixed vegetables
1 T. sesame oil
2 c. cooked white rice
3 T. stir-fry sauce
2 eggs, beaten
4 to 5 chicken breasts, cooked
    and cut into bite-size pieces
3 green onions, thinly sliced

Cook vegetables according to package directions. Meanwhile, preheat a large sauté pan over medium-high heat for 2 to 3 minutes. Add sesame oil and cooked rice to pan. Cook and stir for one minute, until rice is toasted. Stir in sauce. Slowly pour in eggs while stirring rice. Cook and stir for 2 to 4 minutes, until eggs are set. Stir in chicken, vegetables and onions. Cook and stir for 2 to 3 minutes, until heated through. Serves 4 to 6.

When chopping ingredients, be sure not to mix fresh veggies and raw meat on the same cutting board. Use two separate cutting boards, or wash the cutting board well in between ingredients. Don't place cooked food on a plate that has had raw meat on it.

Kids in the *Kitchen*

Honey-Ginger Carrots

Denise Neal
Castle Rock, CO

This is our favorite way to eat cooked carrots...my kids love it! This stovetop version is quick to fix. I like to speed it up even more by buying the carrots already waffle-cut into slices.

1 lb. carrots, peeled and sliced
1/4 t. salt
1/4 c. butter
3 T. honey

1 to 1-1/2 t. fresh ginger, peeled
  and grated
Garnish: chopped fresh parsley

Place carrots in a saucepan; add a small amount of water to just cover carrots. Sprinkle with salt. Cook over medium-high heat just until carrots are tender; drain. Remove from heat. Add butter, honey and ginger; stir until butter and honey are melted. Garnish with chopped parsley. Serves 4.

This is my invariable advice to people: Learn how
to cook...try new recipes, learn from your mistakes,
be fearless, and above all, have fun!
–Julia Child

Chicken Quesadillas

Lori Simmons
Princeville, IL

A very quick dinner to make, only five minutes! Make it your own with Mexican-blend cheese...add crisp bacon instead of chicken, or even just make cheese quesadillas. Let the kids help!

8 6-inch flour tortillas
2 c. cooked chicken, diced
1 c. thick & chunky salsa

1 c. shredded sharp Cheddar
   cheese
4 green onions, chopped

On one-half of each flour tortilla, evenly layer ingredients; fold the other half over. Heat a non-stick skillet over medium-high heat. Cook each quesadilla for 3 minutes on each side, until lightly golden and cheese is melted. Cut into wedges. Serves 4.

Cornbread Muffins Deluxe

Sheila Smith
Roanoke, VA

My son Sherman and I both love these easy-to-make muffins.

1-1/3 c. milk
1/4 c. oil
1 egg, beaten
2 c. self-rising cornmeal
1/4 t. sugar

1/4 c. white onion, diced
1/4 c. green pepper, diced
1/2 to 1 c. shredded sharp
   Cheddar cheese

Combine all ingredients in a bowl; stir well until moistened. Scoop batter by 1/3 cupfuls into greased muffin cups. Bake at 450 degrees for 20 minutes, or until golden. Makes one dozen.

Have kids make up a dinner menu card. Little ones can use crayons and stickers, older kids can use the internet or dictionary to write the menu in another language.

Kids in the *Kitchen*

Lisa's Fresh Salsa

Lori Britt
Bristol, IL

I first tasted this fresh salsa at a party my sister gave. My family loved it! Now we make it all the time. It's great on omelets or scrambled eggs, salads and baked potatoes. It's best when the tomatoes are in season, but you can used canned tomatoes instead. We don't use the jalapeños very often, so if your family doesn't care for spicy food, feel free to leave them out.

4 c. tomatoes, diced
1 c. green onions, diced
1/2 c. green pepper, diced
1/2 c. red pepper, diced
1/2 c. yellow pepper, diced
1 clove garlic, minced

1 T. olive oil
1 T. red wine vinegar
1 t. ground cumin
1 t. salt
Optional: 1 to 4 jalapeño
    peppers, seeded and chopped

In a large bowl, combine tomatoes, onions, peppers and garlic. Add remaining ingredients; toss to mix well. Let stand for one hour at room temperature before serving. Refrigerate any leftovers. Makes about 6-1/2 cups.

Fresh hot peppers are extra flavorful, but make sure that children know to take care when slicing them. It's best to wear rubber gloves, and never touch your eyes until you've washed your hands well.

Mmm-Minestrone

April Jacobs
Loveland, CO

A hearty, veggie-packed hot soup that my family really enjoys when the weather is chilly. The kids all help with chopping the vegetables, so we can put it together in a jiffy.

3 slices bacon, chopped
1/2 c. onion, chopped
1/2 c. celery, chopped
1 clove garlic, minced
1-3/4 c. water
14-1/2 oz. can diced tomatoes
   with Italian seasoning

14-1/2 oz. can beef broth
10-3/4 oz. can bean & bacon
   soup
1 c. zucchini, peeled and diced
1 c. cabbage, chopped
1/2 c. elbow macaroni, uncooked
salt to taste

In a soup pot over medium heat, cook bacon with onion, celery and garlic until bacon is crisp; drain. Add water, tomatoes with juice and remaining ingredients. Bring to a boil; reduce heat to low. Simmer until macaroni is tender, stirring often, about 15 minutes. Serves 6.

Biscuit Buddies

Gregory Bench
Clinton, UT

This recipe was shared by a family member, and I created my own simple version. This super-easy bread has frequented our dinner table ever since!

1/4 c. butter, melted and divided
1 T. Italian seasoning, divided
12-oz. can refrigerated biscuits,
   quartered

1/4 c. grated Parmesan cheese

Add half each of butter and seasoning to an 8"x8" glass baking pan; coat bottom of pan well. Add biscuit pieces to pan in a single layer. Top with remaining butter and seasoning; sprinkle with cheese. Bake at 350 degrees for 15 to 18 minutes, until golden. Serves 4 to 6.

Kids in the *Kitchen*

Southwest Chicken Tortellini Soup

Vicki Lanzendorf
Madison, WI

I found a recipe and altered it to our liking. Now my son Luke says it's his absolute most favorite soup ever.

4 c. chicken broth
1-1/2 c. salsa
1/2 c. carrots, peeled and
   thinly sliced
2 c. cooked chicken, diced

2 c. frozen corn
1/2 c. onion, diced
19-oz. pkg. frozen cheese-filled
   tortellini
5-oz. can evaporated milk

In a soup pot or Dutch oven, combine broth, salsa and carrots. Bring to a boil over medium-high heat; reduce heat to medium. Simmer for about 5 minutes, until carrots are tender. Stir in remaining ingredients except evaporated milk. Cook over medium heat for 10 minutes, stirring often. Stir in milk and heat for one to 2 minutes; do not boil. Makes 6 servings.

Warm soft pretzels can go from oven to table in minutes... it's child's play! Twist strips of refrigerated bread stick dough into pretzel shapes and place on an ungreased baking sheet. Brush with beaten egg white, sprinkle with coarse salt and bake as directed.

Garden Stir-Fry & Sausage

Jody Keiper
Crystal Lake, IL

I plant a garden every year and in mid-August I usually get an abundance of zucchini, tomatoes, green peppers and much more. I use these veggies in as many dishes as I can...this one is a family favorite. For a change, use chicken instead of sausage.

1 to 2 T. olive oil
2 green peppers, cut into chunks
1/2 onion, coarsely chopped
1/2 lb. smoked turkey sausage,
    sliced 1/2-inch thick
1 zucchini or yellow squash,
    sliced

2 tomatoes, cut into chunks
1/4 c. Worcestershire sauce
2 T. soy sauce
1/2 t. honey
pepper to taste
cooked rice or noodles

Heat oil in a large skillet over medium heat. Add peppers, onion and sausage; sauté for about 5 minutes. Add zucchini or squash and cook for 5 minutes, or until vegetables are tender. Add tomatoes, sauces, honey and pepper; heat through. Serve with cooked rice or noodles. Makes 4 to 5 servings.

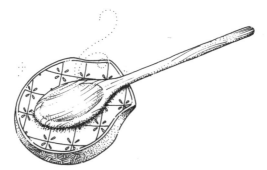

Spoons that are made of metal get hot quickly
when stirring food on the stove...it's best for kids
to use wooden or plastic spoons.

Kids in the *Kitchen*

Easy Dinner In a Foil Packet

Andrea Ford
Montfort, WI

This simple recipe has been in my family for years.
Something about cooking everything all together in foil,
topped with butter, just makes it taste so delicious!

4 ground beef patties
1 onion, thinly sliced
4 carrots, peeled and thinly
  sliced

4 potatoes, peeled and quartered
8 T. butter, sliced into 8 pats
salt and pepper to taste

Cut 4 long pieces of aluminum foil. Place one beef patty on each piece of foil; top each with an onion slice, 1/4 of the carrots and 4 potato quarters. Top each with 2 pats of butter; season with salt and pepper. Pull foil together; fold and seal tightly. Place packets on a baking sheet. Bake at 375 degrees for 1-1/2 hours. Open packets carefully to allow hot steam to escape. Makes 4 servings.

A child of five would understand.
Send someone to fetch a child of five.
–Groucho Marx

Farmers' Market Pasta Salad

Barbara Cebula
Chicopee, MA

I've made this cool pasta salad for many years. Mom used to make it for us as children and we loved it.

2 c. rotini pasta, uncooked
1 c. broccoli, cut into bite-size
  flowerets
1 c. carrots, peeled and sliced
1 c. cherry tomatoes, halved

2 green onions, sliced
16-oz. container low-fat cottage
  cheese
1/2 c. light ranch salad dressing

Cook pasta according to package directions; drain and rinse with cold water. Place pasta in a large bowl; add vegetables and toss to mix. Add cottage cheese and salad dressing; mix lightly. Cover and chill until serving time. Makes 8 servings.

Toss together salads for several days' meals so dinner is ready in a hurry. Store salad greens in a plastic zipping bag, tucking in a paper towel to absorb extra moisture and refrigerate. They'll stay crisp up to four days.

Kids in the *Kitchen*

Becky's Nutty Coleslaw

Becky Drees
Pittsfield, MA

Kids love this fun and fruity summer salad!

3 c. green cabbage, shredded
1 c. purple cabbage
1-1/2 c. carrots, peeled
   and grated
1 c. celery, chopped
1/3 c. crushed pineapple,
   drained

2/3 c. plain yogurt
3 T. honey
2 T. creamy peanut butter
1 T. mayonnaise
1/2 c. honey-roasted peanuts,
   chopped

In a large bowl, combine vegetables and pineapple. Gently stir in yogurt, honey, peanut butter and mayonnaise. Cover and chill until serving time. Just before serving, sprinkle peanuts on top. Makes 8 servings.

Broccoli Salad in a Bag

Karen Van Den Berge
Holland, MI

This is a favorite recipe of mine. It is so easy and takes little time to prepare...great for picnics and everyday meals. Mmm, very tasty! The recipe is easily halved if you aren't feeding a crowd.

8 c. broccoli, cut into bite-size
   flowerets
2 c. cherry tomatoes

1/2 c. onion, sliced
1-1/4 c. Italian salad dressing

Mix all ingredients in a large plastic zipping bag. Seal bag and refrigerate overnight, turning occasionally. Makes 10 to 12 servings.

Be sure to wash fresh produce well under cold water. Firm fruits and vegetables like potatoes can be scrubbed with a veggie brush, while tender varieties like tomatoes and pears can simply be rinsed well.

Alphabet Cookies

Janet Myers
Reading, PA

This is a great recipe for baking with children, as well as a great learning activity. The dough is easy to roll and shape into letters, numbers or shapes. Afterwards, they can eat their creations!

1 c. butter, softened
1-1/2 c. plus 3 T. sugar, divided
2 eggs, beaten
3 c. all-purpose flour

2 t. baking powder
1 t. baking soda
1/2 t. salt
2 t. cinnamon, divided

In a large bowl, combine butter and 1-1/2 cups sugar. Beat with an electric mixer on medium speed until light and fluffy. Add eggs; beat until blended. Sift flour, baking powder, baking soda, salt and 1/2 teaspoon cinnamon over butter mixture. Mix with a wooden spoon until a stiff dough forms. Cover and refrigerate at least 2 hours. When ready to bake, divide dough into 4 portions; divide each portion into 12 walnut-size pieces. Roll each piece of dough into a rope, 5 to 6 inches long. Form ropes into letters, numbers or other shapes as desired. Place cookies on greased baking sheets, about 2 inches apart. In a small bowl, combine remaining sugar and cinnamon; sprinkle over cookies. Bake at 350 degrees for 13 to 15 minutes, until golden. Remove cookies to wire racks; let cool completely. Makes 4 dozen.

Baking together is a fun family activity and a great choice for kids just starting to learn how to cook. As you measure, mix and bake together, be sure to share any stories about hand-me-down recipes...you'll be creating memories as well as sweet treats!

Kids in the *Kitchen*

Anytime Baked Apples

James Bohner
Harrisburg, PA

These delicious apples are perfect for breakfast, brunch or anytime. The brown sugar mixture is easy for kids to stir up. Garnish with your favorite nuts, raisins or dried cranberries!

6 apples	1 t. apple pie spice
1/2 c. brown sugar, packed	1 t. cinnamon
2 T. butter, softened	1/2 t. salt

Peel apples, if desired. Core apples from the top; do not cut through to the bottom. Arrange apples in an ungreased casserole dish. Combine remaining ingredients in a small bowl; mix with a fork until crumbly. Spoon brown sugar mixture into and over the apples. Bake, uncovered, at 375 degrees for 30 minutes, or until apples are fork-tender. Serve warm. Makes 6 servings.

If you have little ones, remember that hot pans should be kept where they can't be reached. Always turn saucepan handles on the stove away from the edge.

Ice Cream in a Bag

Hope Davenport
Portland, TX

My kids love this yummy ice cream. It is fun to make and everyone can be involved in making it. We pass it from person to person until the ice cream is ready to eat.

1 c. whole milk
1 t. vanilla extract
2 T. sugar
1-qt. heavy-duty plastic zipping
   bag with slide closure

1-gal. heavy-duty plastic zipping
   bag with slide closure
1/4 c. rock salt
4 c. cracked ice

Pour milk, vanilla and sugar into the one-quart plastic bag. Squeeze as much air out of the bag as possible; seal tightly. Place small bag into the one-gallon bag; cover with ice and rock salt. Seal large bag tightly. Shake and flip the large bag for about 10 minutes. If it gets too cold to handle, wrap with a towel. Don't open large bag to check the ice cream, because it may not seal properly afterwards. After 10 minutes, open both bags; spoon ice cream into small cups. Makes 4 servings.

Variations:

Instead of vanilla extract: use a different extract flavor.

Omit the vanilla and half the sugar: add some chocolate or strawberry syrup to the milk mixture.

When kids come to the grocery store with you, let them help you shop for family meals. It's a great chance to teach them about comparing package sizes, prices and other lessons about making dinner.

194

Sweet TREATS

Banana-Chocolate Chip Snack Cakes

*Sheri Graham
Moundridge, KS*

*My kids love to snack, and finding healthy snacks for them is a
challenge. One day I came up with this recipe when I had some
ripe bananas to use up. It was a big hit...my kids love them!*

3 eggs
1 c. ripe bananas, mashed
2 c. milk
1/2 c. water
1-1/2 T. honey
6 T. olive oil

3-1/2 c. whole-wheat flour
3 T. baking powder
1 t. sea salt
6-oz. pkg. semi-sweet chocolate
  chips

Beat eggs in a large bowl. Add remaining ingredients except chocolate
chips; mix well. Add a bit more water if batter is too thick. Heat a
buttered griddle over medium heat. Working in batches, drop batter
onto griddle by tablespoonfuls. Cook until golden on the bottom. Top
with a few chocolate chips; turn and cook other side. Cool on a wire
rack. If not serving right away, freeze or refrigerate; microwave briefly
to warm. Makes about 5 dozen.

Bake up some cupcake cones for a school party. Prepare
a cake mix and fill 24 flat-bottom cones 2/3 full of batter.
Set the cones in muffin tins and bake as package directs
for cupcakes. Cool, then top with frosting and lots of
candy sprinkles. Kids will love 'em!

Sweet Treats

Chocolate-Zucchini Snack Cake

Jenny Bishoff
Mountain Lake Park, MD

I had tons of zucchini, and my kids were bored with regular zucchini bread. So I combined several recipes to come up with this delicious treat...they like it and you will too!

16-1/2 oz. pkg. devil's food
   cake mix
2 eggs
1/4 c. oil
1/2 c. milk

2 c. zucchini, peeled and
   shredded
12-oz. pkg. semi-sweet
   chocolate chips, divided

In a large bowl, combine all ingredients except chocolate chips. Beat with an electric mixer on high speed for 2 minutes. Stir in half of the chocolate chips. Divide batter between 2 greased 8"x8" baking pans. Sprinkle remaining chocolate chips over batter. Bake at 350 degrees for 30 to 35 minutes. Cool; cut into squares. Makes 2 dozen.

Black Bean Brownies

Catherine Laughlin
Wichita, KS

You will never believe there are beans in these moist brownies! I gave this recipe to my sons, who ate lots of black beans during the two-year missions they served in Brazil. Little kids just love them too!

15-oz. can black beans, drained
   and rinsed
18-oz. pkg. brownie mix

1/2 c. water
Optional: chocolate chips or
   flaked coconut

Mash beans well, with a food processor if possible. Combine beans, dry brownie mix and water in a bowl; stir until well blended. Spread in a greased 8"x8" baking pan. If desired, sprinkle with chocolate chips or coconut. Bake at 325 degrees for about 50 minutes, until a toothpick tests clean. Cut into squares. Serves 8.

Pumpkin Oatmeal Scotchies

Kristy Markners
Fort Mill, SC

Oatmeal scotchies are my husband's favorite cookie. This is my healthier version...our kids Kaleb and Makenzy love them!

1-1/4 c. all-purpose flour
1 t. baking soda
1/2 t. cinnamon
1/2 c. butter, softened
1/2 c. canned pumpkin
3/4 c. sugar
3/4 c. brown sugar, packed

1 T. flax seed
1 egg, beaten
3 T. water
1 t. vanilla extract
1 c. butterscotch chips
3 c. long-cooking oats, uncooked

Combine flour, baking soda and cinnamon; set aside. In a separate bowl, remaining ingredients except butterscotch chips and oats; mix well. Gradually stir in flour mixture; fold in butterscotch chips and oats. Spoon dough by heaping teaspoonfuls onto parchment paper-lined baking sheets. Bake at 375 degrees for 9 to 12 minutes, until golden. Makes 4 dozen.

Plastic zipping bags are handy for piping frosting onto cookies. Fill a small bag with frosting and seal, then snip off a tiny corner...frosting will squeeze out easily. Afterwards, just toss away the bag.

Sweet Treats

Good-for-You Cookies

Janis Parr
Campbellford, Ontario

Kids gobble up these tasty cookies, never guessing
how nutritious they are!

1 c. butter, softened
1 c. brown sugar, packed
1/2 c. honey
2 eggs, beaten
1 t. vanilla extract
1 c. long-cooking oats,
  uncooked

1 c. whole-wheat flour
1/2 c. all-purpose flour
1 t. baking soda
1/2 t. salt
1 c. raisins
1/2 c. wheat germ
1/2 c. sunflower kernels

Blend together butter, brown sugar, honey, eggs and vanilla. Add remaining ingredients; mix well. Drop by tablespoonfuls onto greased or parchment paper-lined baking sheets, 2 inches apart. Bake at 350 degrees for 10 to 12 minutes, until lightly golden. Cool; store in an airtight container. Makes 4 dozen.

Peanut Butter Cookies in a Wink

Lynnette Rohde
Holiday, FL

This is a very simple recipe my son and I would make together
after a busy "little school dude and single working mom"
crazy day...warm, fast and fresh flourless cookies!

1 c. creamy peanut butter
1 c. sugar

1 egg, beaten
1 t. baking soda

Mix together all ingredients until well blended. Roll dough into one-inch balls; place on ungreased baking sheets. Bake at 325 degrees for 8 to 10 minutes. Remove from oven; cool on baking sheets until set, about 5 minutes. Remove cookies to wire racks to finish cooling. Makes 3 dozen.

Honey Whole-Wheat Date Muffins

Eleanor Dionne
Beverly, MA

Kids love these chewy-topped muffins! My granddaughters can eat two or three at one sitting.

1 egg, beaten
1/2 c. milk
1/4 c. canola oil
3/4 c. whole-wheat flour
3/4 c. all-purpose flour
1/2 c. sugar

2 t. baking powder
1/2 t. salt
Optional: 2 T. bran
3/4 c. chopped dates
Garnish: honey in squeeze bottle

Beat together egg, milk and oil; set aside. In a separate large bowl, combine flours, sugar, baking powder, salt and bran, if using. Make a well in center of flour mixture. Add egg mixture and dates to well; stir just until moistened. Spoon batter into 8 greased muffin cups, filling 2/3 full. Bake at 400 degrees for 20 to 25 minutes. Remove from oven; immediately drizzle generously with honey. Makes 8 muffins.

A slick trick when baking muffins! Grease muffin cups
on the bottoms and just halfway up the sides...
muffins will bake up nicely domed on top.

Sweet Treats

Edith's Banana Muffins

Diana Krol
Nickerson, KS

My dear neighbor baked banana bread for her son every week. Whenever my kids smelled it baking, they would run for her back door...she never sent them home empty-handed! Imagine my kids' surprise the first time I baked it at our home...they had no idea I was capable! This recipe remains their favorite, and is now the favorite of my grandchildren too.

2/3 c. sugar
1/4 c. butter, softened
2 eggs, beaten
3 to 4 ripe bananas, mashed
1 t. baking soda

2 c. all-purpose flour
1/2 c. mini semi-sweet
　　chocolate chips
Optional: 1/2 c. chopped nuts

Blend sugar into butter; stir in eggs, then bananas. Beat in baking soda; add flour and stir until moistened. Fold in chocolate chips and nuts, if using. Spoon batter into 24 greased muffin cups, filling 2/3 full. Bake at 350 degrees for about 20 minutes, until golden. Turn out muffins; serve warm or cooled. Makes 2 dozen.

Carrot Cake Muffins

Becky Danielson
Hayesville, NC

My kids love these quick and nutritious muffins. They're a great treat after supper with a glass of milk. For a richer treat, substitute devil's food cake mix for the carrot cake mix.

15-1/4 oz. pkg. carrot cake mix   15-oz. can pumpkin

Add dry cake mix to a large bowl. Add pumpkin; stir until well mixed. Line a muffin tin with paper liners; spray with non-stick vegetable spray. Spoon batter into 18 muffin cups, filling 2/3 full. Bake at 350 degrees for 14 to 18 minutes, until muffins test done with a toothpick. Remove to a wire rack; cool. Makes 1-1/2 dozen.

Chewy Maple-Oat Clusters

Hannah Hopkins
Plainfield, VT

When your hungry kids raid the kitchen after school,
this crunchy treat is a delicious and healthy option!

1-1/2 c. long-cooking oats,
   uncooked
1 c. crispy rice cereal
1 c. bran flake cereal
1/2 c. pecan halves, cut in half
1/2 c. sunflower kernels

1/2 c. raisins
8-oz. pkg. mixed dried fruit,
   chopped
1/4 c. butter, melted
1-1/2 c. pure maple syrup

Spread oats in a lightly greased 13"x9" baking pan. Bake, stirring occasionally, at 325 degrees for 20 to 30 minutes, until lightly golden. Stir in cereals, pecans and sunflower seeds. Continue baking for 14 to 16 minutes, until lightly toasted. Remove from oven; stir in raisins and fruit. In a small bowl, stir together butter and syrup; drizzle over cereal mixture. Stir to coat well. Return to oven, stirring occasionally, for 45 to 50 minutes, until mixture clumps together. Spread on wax paper; break into pieces. Store in an airtight container. Makes 8 cups.

Turn a metal cookie sheet into a family message center... spray on craft paint in a cheerful color. Attach a ribbon hanger and use magnets to hold notes and reminders.

Sweet Treats

Best Chocolate Chip Cookies
Samantha Reilly
Gig Harbor, WA

This is my family's favorite cookie recipe! We often end up eating at least half of the dough, as it's almost as good that way. Just follow the directions below.

1-1/2 c. butter, softened
1 c. sugar
1 c. brown sugar, packed
3 eggs, beaten
1-1/2 t. vanilla extract
3-1/2 c. all-purpose flour
2 t. baking powder
1-1/2 t. salt
12-oz. pkg. semi-sweet
   chocolate chips

In a large bowl, blend together butter and sugars; stir in eggs and vanilla. In a separate bowl, mix together flour, baking powder and salt. Gradually add flour mixture to butter mixture; mix well. Fold in chocolate chips. Spoon dough by heaping tablespoonfuls onto ungreased baking sheets. Bake at 350 degrees for 10 to 12 minutes for chewy cookies, 12 to 13 minutes for soft cookies or 14 to 15 minutes for crunchy cookies. Cool on wire racks. Makes 2 dozen.

For edible dough: Mix as above; omit eggs and add 3 tablespoons water. Keep refrigerated.

For perfect round cookies: Mix as above; increase flour to 4 cups. On a well-floured surface, roll out dough as for sugar cookies. Cut with a round cutter; bake as above.

A small ice cream scoop is so handy when making drop cookies...just scoop the dough from the bowl and release it onto the cookie sheet. So easy!

Mom's Chocolate Chip-Oat Cookies

Lisa Hains
Jordan, Ontario

I thought I'd share my mom's cookie recipe with you. It has more of a shortbread texture. It's a little healthier, made with oats and with less sugar than most. It also has no eggs, so it's perfect for folks who must avoid eggs. But we just love it because it's delicious!

1 c. butter, softened
1 c. brown sugar, packed
1 t. baking soda
1 t. vanilla extract
1/4 c. hot water
2 c. quick-cooking oats, uncooked

2 c. all-purpose flour
1 t. salt
1/2 c. semi-sweet chocolate chips
Optional: 1/2 c. chopped walnuts
Optional: 1/4 c. dried cranberries or cherries

In a large bowl, blend together butter and brown sugar. In a separate bowl, stir together baking soda, vanilla and hot water; add to butter mixture. Stir in oats, flour and salt. Fold in chocolate chips; add walnuts and/or fruit, if using. Drop by tablespoonfuls onto lightly greased baking sheets. Bake at 350 degrees for 10 minutes, or until edges are just beginning to turn golden. Cool on wire racks. Makes 3-1/2 to 4 dozen.

Enjoy fresh-baked cookies in minutes by freezing some of your cookie dough! Simply drop rounded spoonfuls on a parchment-lined baking sheet, freeze until firm and transfer to a plastic zipping bag. When you're ready to bake, just add a few extra minutes of baking time.

Sweet Treats

Anything Drop Cookies

Diane Spencer
Quesnel, British Columbia

Mom & Dad ran a foster home for many years, with kids of all ages coming & going all the time. Mom used to make these cookies daily and they tasted different almost every time...they could be made using practically anything she had in her pantry. Good memories!

1 c. all-purpose flour
1/2 t. baking powder
1/8 t. baking soda
1/4 t. salt
1/3 c. butter, softened
1/3 c. brown sugar, packed

1 egg, beaten
1-1/2 T. milk
1/2 t. vanilla extract
3/4 c. chopped walnuts
3/4 c. semi-sweet chocolate
 chips

Combine flour, baking powder, baking soda and salt; set aside. In a separate bowl, blend together butter and brown sugar. Add egg, milk and vanilla; mix well. Gradually add flour mixture to butter mixture, beating well after each addition. Fold in walnuts and chocolate chips. Drop by teaspoonfuls onto greased baking sheets, 2 inches apart. Bake at 375 degrees until lightly golden, about 10 minutes. Cool on wire racks. Makes 2 dozen.

Variations:

Instead of vanilla extract: use almond, peppermint or maple extract.

Instead of chopped walnuts: use chopped almonds, pecans or hazelnuts, or flaked coconut.

Instead of chocolate chips: use white chocolate, peanut butter or butterscotch chips.

Make up some bite-size ice cream treats... sandwich a scoop of softened ice cream between small cookies.

Debbie's Oat & Nut Cookies

Debbie Blundi
Kunkletown, PA

*These cookies are a big hit with our grandkids Kaleb and Brayden...
they like to help mash the bananas! My husband and I have helped
them to grow their own sections in our veggie garden and then use
what they harvest. They love to be in the kitchen with "Mom-Mom"
coming up with new recipes. These cookies are free of sugar, dairy,
fat, soy and gluten.*

1/3 c. peanut, almond, cashew
   or sunflower butter
3 ripe bananas, mashed
2 T. unsweetened non-dairy
   milk
1/2 t. cinnamon

1 t. vanilla extract
1/4 c. Date Paste (below)
2-1/2 c. quick-cooking oats,
   uncooked
1/4 to 3/4 c. gluten-free baking
   mix

Combine all ingredients in a large bowl. Mix well with your hands,
adding more baking mix as needed to form a dough consistency. Form
dough into balls by teaspoonfuls; place on ungreased baking sheets.
With the back of a fork, slightly flatten balls and make decorative
indents. Bake at 350 degrees for 13 minutes, or until lightly golden.
Makes about one dozen.

Date Paste:

2 c. pitted dates

1/2 c. water or non-dairy milk

Place dates in a blender. Process until creamy, adding water or milk as
necessary until smooth. Cover and refrigerate up to 2 weeks. May be
used in place of sugar in almost any recipe.

Wrap up a batch of your
favorite cookies and have
the kids deliver them to the
teachers' lounge at school...
they're sure to be appreciated!

Sweet Treats

Sugar-Free Banana Cookies

Susan McDaniel
Kent, WA

I used to work in a family resource center and I made these cookies for the children at our events. The parents liked the idea of a sugar-free cookie...the kids just liked getting a cookie!

3 ripe bananas
2 c. quick-cooking oats,
   uncooked

1 c. chopped dates
1/3 c. oil
1 t. vanilla extract

Mash bananas in a large bowl. Stir in oats, dates, oil and vanilla; let stand 15 minutes. Drop by teaspoonfuls onto ungreased baking sheets; press down lightly with a fork. Bake at 350 degrees for 20 minutes. For best flavor, serve within one to 2 days. Makes 2 dozen.

Forgotten Cookies

Wendy McDonald
Glendale, AZ

Our family has been enjoying these flourless cookies for over ten years. I think you'll love them too!

2 egg whites, room temperature
3/4 c. sugar
1/8 t. salt
1 t. vanilla extract

1 c. mini semi-sweet
   chocolate chips
Optional: 1 c. chopped pecans

Preheat oven to 350 degrees. Beat egg whites with an electric mixer on high speed until foamy. Gradually add sugar, beating until stiff peaks form. Stir in remaining ingredients. Drop by teaspoonfuls onto ungreased aluminum foil-lined baking sheets. Place baking sheets in oven; immediately turn oven off and allow to cool. Leave cookies in closed oven overnight. Makes about 4 dozen.

Use an oven thermometer to check baking temperatures... no more burnt or underdone cookies.

Eric's Apple Squares

Molly Ebert
Columbus, IN

When my son Eric was a teenager, these tasty fruit-filled squares were a huge favorite with him and his buddies. When they rolled in after school, a platter of Apple Squares and a tall glass of milk waiting on the table made me the favorite mom of the neighborhood!

1/2 c. butter, melted
1 c. brown sugar, packed
1 c. plus 2 T. sugar, divided
2 eggs, beaten
2 t. vanilla extract
2 c. all-purpose flour

2 t. baking powder
1/2 t. salt
1 c. apple, peeled, cored
    and diced
1/2 t. cinnamon

Add melted butter to a large bowl; stir in brown sugar, one cup sugar, eggs and vanilla. Add flour, baking powder, salt and apple; mix well. Pour batter into a greased 8"x8" baking pan. Combine cinnamon and remaining sugar; sprinkle over batter. Bake at 350 degrees for 30 minutes. Cool; cut into squares. Makes 1-1/4 dozen.

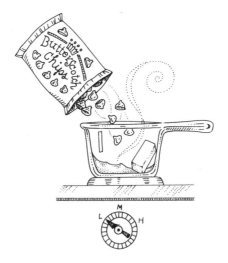

Create a heavenly glaze for any apple dessert. Melt together
1/2 cup butterscotch chips, 2 tablespoons butter and
2 tablespoons whipping cream over low heat.

Sweet Treats

Pineapple Bars

Carol Murnan
Brook Park, OH

My mom got this recipe in the 1970s from her neighbors. They were Italian and loved to cook! These bars were served at a summer picnic, and were a hit with everyone. Mom was lucky enough to get the recipe...they are so moist and delicious!

1 c. butter, softened
2 c. sugar
4 eggs
1-1/2 c. all-purpose flour
1/2 t. baking soda

1/2 t. salt
2-1/2 c. crushed pineapple,
   very well-drained
1/2 c. chopped nuts
Garnish: powdered sugar

In a large bowl, blend butter, sugar and eggs, adding one egg at a time. Beat in flour, baking soda and salt. Stir in pineapple gradually, distributing it evenly throughout the batter. Stir in nuts. Spread batter in a greased 13"x9" baking pan. Bake at 350 degrees for 35 to 40 minutes. Cool in pan for 10 to 15 minutes. Sprinkle with powdered sugar; cut into squares. Makes 16 to 20 bars.

Sugar Cookie Dough

Everyone loves a dessert pizza! Press ready-made sugar cookie dough into an ungreased pizza pan and bake as directed. Let crust cool, then spread with a mixture of an 8-ounce package cream cheese, one cup sugar and one teaspoon vanilla. Top with fresh fruit and cut into wedges.

Blastin' Blueberry Crunch

Marsha Baker
Pioneer, OH

I first made this tasty dessert as a newlywed. I remember taking it on a camping trip when our kids were small. It's easy and the oatmeal topping adds a wonderful crunch.

1-1/2 c. quick-cooking oats, uncooked
1 c. all-purpose flour
3/4 to 1 c. brown sugar, packed
1/2 c. butter, melted
1/2 t. cinnamon
Optional: 1/4 t. salt
1/2 c. sugar

1 T. plus 1/8 t. cornstarch
3/4 c. water
2 T. lemon juice
1 t. vanilla extract
3 to 4 c. fresh or frozen blueberries
Garnish: ice cream

In a large bowl, combine oats, flour, brown sugar, butter, cinnamon and salt, if using; mix well. Spread half of oat mixture in the bottom of a greased 8"x8" baking pan; set aside. In a saucepan over medium heat, combine sugar and cornstarch; add water and lemon juice. Bring to a boil; boil until thick, stirring constantly. Stir in vanilla and blueberries. Pour over oat mixture. Sprinkle remaining oat mixture over top. Bake at 350 degrees for 40 to 45 minutes. Cut into squares; serve warm, topped with ice cream. Makes 8 servings.

Top your best homemade desserts with real whipped cream... it's simple. With an electric mixer on high speed, beat one cup whipping cream until soft peaks form. Add one tablespoon powdered sugar and one teaspoon vanilla extract. Continue to beat until stiff peaks form.

Sweet Treats

German Apple Cake

Lori Peterson
Effingham, KS

This cake is my mom's all-time favorite. She has been making it as long as I can remember. Now I carry on the tradition for my kids.

3 eggs
1 c. oil
2 c. sugar
2 c. all-purpose flour
1 t. baking soda
1/4 t. salt

1 t. cinnamon
1-1/2 t. vanilla extract
4 c. apples, peeled, cored and
    diced
1 c. chopped pecans

Beat eggs and oil until foamy; stir in sugar. Mix in flour, baking soda, salt, cinnamon and vanilla. Fold in apples and pecans. Spread batter in a greased 13"x9" baking pan. Bake at 325 degrees for one hour, or until a toothpick tests clean. Spread cooled cake with Cream Cheese Frosting; cut into squares. Makes 12 to 15 servings.

Cream Cheese Frosting:

3 T. butter, melted
8-oz. cream cheese, softened

2 t. vanilla extract
2-1/2 c. powdered sugar

With an electric mixer on low speed, beat butter, cream cheese and vanilla until smooth. Gradually beat in powdered sugar until smooth.

Making dessert for a crowd? It's tricky to successfully double or triple recipe ingredients for cakes or cookies. Instead, choose a recipe that feeds a bunch, or prepare several batches of a single recipe until you have the quantity you need.

Quickie Monster Bars

Lisa Cameron
Twin Falls, ID

My family absolutely loves these delicious bar cookies. You will too! It's a very quick recipe perfect for school bake sales, potlucks and family gatherings, or just a fast after-school snack. You can substitute raisins, butterscotch chips, flaked coconut...there are endless possibilities.

1/2 c. butter, softened
1 c. sugar
1 c. brown sugar, packed
1 c. creamy peanut butter
1/2 c. crunchy peanut butter
3 eggs, room temperature
1 t. vanilla extract

2 t. baking soda
4-1/2 c. long-cooking oats, uncooked
1 c. candy-coated chocolates
3/4 c. mini semi-sweet chocolate chips

In a large bowl, blend together butter, sugars, peanut butters, eggs, vanilla and baking soda. Add oats and mix well. Fold in chocolates and chocolate chips. Spray a 15"x10" jelly-roll pan with non-stick vegetable spray. Spread batter evenly in pan. Bake at 350 degrees for 20 minutes. Cool completely; cut into bars. Makes 2 dozen.

Out of brown sugar? You can substitute an equal amount of white sugar for all or some of the brown sugar called for in a recipe. Or improvise by adding 1-1/2 teaspoons of molasses to one cup of white sugar to make light brown sugar.

Sweet Treats

Monkey Bites

Tonya Ashcraft
Weatherford, OK

I used to make this recipe when my kids were little. The kids would start to act like monkeys, jumping around and being silly...it was so funny to watch them! Now that they are grown, every now & then we still talk about how much fun we had laughing together over a batch of Monkey Bites.

14-oz. pkg. banana-nut muffin
   & quick bread mix
1/4 c. sugar
1/4 c. oil
2 eggs, beaten

1/4 c. strained banana
   baby food
3/4 c. semi-sweet chocolate
   chunks
2/3 c. chopped walnuts

In a bowl, combine dry muffin mix, sugar, oil, eggs and baby food; stir until well mixed. Stir in chocolate chunks and walnuts. Spray 2 baking sheets with non-stick vegetable spray. Drop dough onto baking sheets by heaping tablespoonfuls, spacing 2 inches apart. Bake at 400 degrees for 11 to 13 minutes, until lightly golden. Makes 2 dozen.

Whip up some ice cream pops for the kids! Place scoops of ice cream on a baking sheet. Insert wooden treat sticks and freeze for 2 hours. Roll in candy sprinkles and serve right away, or return to the freezer to enjoy later.

Magic Cookie Bar Pie

Jenn Erickson
Pacific Grove, CA

The easiest pie ever...the most delicious too! Can't decide between cookies or pie? This is the dessert for you. Hands busy with crafting and need to enlist some child labor? Even your kindergartner can help make this recipe. Clean-up is a snap too...no bowls to wash. Now that's sweet!

14-oz. can sweetened
   condensed milk
9-inch graham cracker crust
2/3 c. butterscotch chips

1 c. sweetened flaked coconut
3/4 c. finely chopped pecans
   or walnuts
1 c. semi-sweet chocolate chips

Spread condensed milk evenly into crust. Layer with remaining ingredients in the order listed. Place pie plate on a baking sheet to allow the pie to bake evenly. Bake at 350 degrees for 35 minutes, or until edges are golden and bubbly. Set pie on a wire rack; cool to room temperature for several hours. Cut into wedges. Makes 8 servings.

I don't think a really good pie can be made without
a dozen or so children peeking over your shoulder
as you stoop to look in at it every little while.
–John Gould

Sweet Treats

Bryson's Peanut Butter Pie

Shonnie Sims
Canton, GA

*My kids just love this wonderful easy-to-make pie! It's named
for my youngest son, because right after dinner he would
always ask, where is my peanut butter pie?*

8-oz. cream cheese, softened
1 c. powdered sugar
1/2 c. creamy peanut butter
2 T. milk
8-oz. container frozen whipped
   topping, thawed

9-inch graham cracker crust
Garnish: crushed peanut butter
   cups, chocolate syrup

In a large bowl, blend cream cheese and powered sugar. Stir in peanut
butter and milk. Fold in whipped topping; spoon mixture into pie crust.
Cover and chill. Top with crushed peanut butter cups; drizzle with
chocolate syrup. Cut into wedges. Makes 8 servings.

Invite family & friends to an Un-Birthday Party. Serve
everyone's favorite foods, wear party hats, play games like
"Pin the Tail on the Donkey" and have a silly gift for each
person to unwrap. Everyone is sure to have a delightful time!

Beckie's Mug of Joy

Beckie Apple
Grannis, AR

Chocolatey cake that's ready in a few moments...it's our secret!
Or wrap the dry ingredients in a little bag, tie on the directions
and tuck into a pretty mug for a sure-to-be-appreciated gift.

1/4 c. self-rising flour
1/4 c. sugar
2 T. baking cocoa
1/4 c. mayonnaise

3 drops vanilla extract
Optional: 2 t. mini chocolate
   chips, chopped nuts or
   flaked coconut

Place flour, sugar and cocoa in a large microwave-safe coffee mug;
mix well with a fork. Add mayonnaise and vanilla; mix well. Stir in
optional ingredients, if desired. Microwave on high setting for
3 minutes; cake will rise and then fall. Let stand in microwave for
2 minutes. While cake is still hot, slip a knife along the sides and slide
cake onto a plate. Serves one.

Fudgy Chocolate Pots

Husna Haq
Tully, NY

This is how I unwind after a long day...I bake two fudgy chocolate
pots and curl up with my favorite book. By the time I scrape up the
last moist bits, I'm transported. I call it chocolate magic!

6 T. semi-sweet chocolate chips
1/4 c. butter, sliced
6 T. sugar

1-1/2 T. all-purpose flour
1 egg, beaten

Combine chocolate chips and butter in a microwave-proof bowl.
Microwave on high setting for one minute, or until butter is melted.
Stir until blended. Mix in sugar and flour; stir in egg. Divide batter
between 2 buttered ramekins. Bake at 400 degrees for 20 minutes.
Serve warm. Makes 2 servings.

Sweet Treats

Apple Crisp in a Mug

Abi Buening
Grand Forks, ND

Looking for a quick dessert...like, right now?
This is yummy, and it'll be your little secret!

2 apples, peeled, cored
  and sliced
2 T. sugar
1/2 c. quick-cooking oats,
  uncooked

3 T. brown sugar, packed
2 T. all-purpose flour
2 T. butter, softened
1/2 t. cinnamon
Garnish: vanilla ice cream

Spray a large microwave-safe mug with non-stick vegetable spray. Add apple slices; sprinkle with sugar. Mix oats, brown sugar, flour, butter and cinnamon until crumbly; add to mug. Microwave on high for 5 to 6 minutes. Top with ice cream. Serves one.

Bananas Foster for Two

Beth Kramer
Port Saint Lucie, FL

After the kids have gone to bed, I stir up this luscious treat in
a jiffy...it makes just enough for myself and a friend!

2 T. butter, sliced
1-1/2 T. brown sugar, packed
2 ripe bananas, sliced diagonally

1-1/2 t. dark rum, or
  1/2 t. rum extract
Garnish: vanilla ice cream

In a skillet over medium heat, bring butter, brown sugar and bananas just to a boil. Cook and stir for 2 minutes. Add rum or extract; cook and stir for 30 seconds. To serve, spoon over a scoop of ice cream. Serves two.

Create a cozy nook for yourself!
A comfy chair and a table provide a
quiet place for you to relax and
read a book, enjoy a treat or
just make a grocery list.

Index

Index

Index

YOUR recipe could appear in our next cookbook!

Share your tried & true family favorites with us instantly at

www.gooseberrypatch.com

If you'd rather jot 'em down by hand, just mail this form to...

Gooseberry Patch • Cookbooks – Call for Recipes
2545 Farmers Dr., #380 • Columbus, OH 43235

If your recipe is selected for a book, you'll receive a FREE copy!

Please share only your original recipes or those that you have made your own over the years.

Recipe Name:

Number of Servings:

Any fond memories about this recipe? Special touches you like to add
or handy shortcuts?

Ingredients (include specific measurements):

Instructions (continue on back if needed):

Special Code: **cookbookspage**

Over ➤

Extra space for recipe if needed:

Tell us about yourself...

Your complete contact information is needed so that we can send you your FREE cookbook, if your recipe is published. Phone numbers and email addresses are kept private and will only be used if we have questions about your recipe.

Name:

Address:

City: State: Zip:

Email:

Daytime Phone:

Thank you! Vickie & Jo Ann

Your exclusive ticket to

a Gooseberry Patch adventure!

When a new season is drawing near, there's nothing more exciting than pulling out favorite recipes and getting inspired. As an **exclusive, free gift** for Gooseberry Patch email subscribers, Vickie and JoAnn are creating **limited edition collections** of the very best of the seasons.

These handcrafted seasonal guides (**$9.95 value**) are full of our favorite recipes, inspiring photos, DIY tips and holiday ideas – you'll be celebrating all season long! A new issue will be released 4 times per year and each one is available for a limited time only.

If you haven't signed up yet, come aboard. Your subscription is your ticket to year 'round inspiration – and it's completely free!

www.gooseberrypatch.com/signup

Visit our website today, add your name to our email list, and you'll be able to download our latest seasonal preview instantly!

Find Gooseberry Patch
wherever you are!

www.gooseberrypatch.com

Call us toll-free at 1·800·854·6673